PRAISE FOR *RECLAIM YOUR MIND*

"*Reclaim Your Mind* is both a manifesto and a manual for how to navigate our relationship with our digital devices. Informed by a deep contemplative practice and a genuine appreciation for technology, Jay Vidyarthi weaves together a tapestry of wisdom that will benefit all of us in the modern world."
—Richard J. Davidson, *New York Times* bestselling author of *The Emotional Life of Your Brain*

"Jay has written a wise and compelling compendium supporting common sense and scientific reasoning in a time of emotionally charged and polarizing narratives. He's talking about harnessing technology to prevent and mitigate harm. This book is about nothing less than recruiting contemplative contentment in the service of improving world happiness, broadly considered and at scale. Definitely a read for our time."
—Shinzen Young, author of *The Science of Enlightenment* and creator of the Unified Mindfulness system

"If you need help protecting your attention in a world seemingly intent on stealing it, look no further: Jay is a trustworthy and empathetic guide whose new book is packed with practical, mindfulness-inspired advice. *Reclaim Your Mind* will come as a relief to anyone who's feeling guilty and helpless about their screen time."

—Catherine Price, author of *How to Break Up with Your Phone* and *The Power of Fun*

"If you want to live a sovereign life, one in which you are in the driver's seat rather than conditioned by technology, read this book. Jay is a tech insider and mindfulness expert intent on giving you back your freedom."

—Emma Seppala, PhD, Yale faculty; author of *Sovereign: Reclaim Your Freedom, Energy, and Power in a Time of Distraction, Uncertainty, and Chaos*

"*Reclaim Your Mind* is a wonderful book to help us develop a mindful relationship to digital devices, giving us practical insights to free us from the algorithms of craving. Highly recommend!"

—Loch Kelly, MDiv, LCSW; creator of the Mindful Glimpses app; nondual mindfulness teacher; author; and psychotherapist

"A much-needed meditation on modernity."

—Vince Fakhoury Horn, cofounder of Buddhist Geeks and Interbeing, Inc.

"In an age of digital overwhelm, *Reclaim Your Mind* offers a refreshingly balanced perspective on the complex relationship we have with our devices. Drawing on his deep expertise as one of the world's leading designers of mindful tech, Vidyarthi offers a wise and practical roadmap to navigating the digital landscape. His book is a must-read for anyone seeking more balance in our hyper-connected world."

—Cortland Dahl, PhD; author of *A Meditator's Guide to Buddhism* and creator of the Healthy Minds Program app

"*Reclaim Your Mind* is the antidote we need for the toxic relationship so many of us have with technology—a relationship that steals our attention and strains our connections with others. Jay Vidyarthi's book is a refreshing reminder that we each have the power to take control of our minds and build healthy relationships with anything in life, even technology. With practical advice and relatable tools, this book empowers readers to cultivate habits that not only nourish their mind and body but also strengthen families, communities, and workplaces."

—Scott Snibbe, author of *How to Train a Happy Mind*, new media artist, computer scientist, and entrepreneur

"Jay Vidyarthi brilliantly combines his expertise in technology and mindfulness, offering lighthearted, practical strategies that are relatable and resonate deeply in our tech-saturated world. A must-read for anyone seeking to cultivate a healthier relationship with technology."

—David Vago, PhD; neuroscientist at Brigham and Women's Hospital, Harvard Medical School; president of the International Society for Contemplative Research; and Mind & Life Institute fellow

"A well-crafted and timely guide for navigating challenges of the digital age... By providing readers with small, realistic steps, [Vidyarthi] allows even the most tech-dependent person to create some breathing room in their life. A gentle, well-organized how-to guide to interacting with tech in a healthier way."
—*Kirkus Reviews*

"Authentic, relatable, and profoundly inspiring, *Reclaim Your Mind* is more than just a must-read—it's a transformative guide to reclaiming control in our digital age. Packed with actionable insights, I am sharing it with my entire network!"
—Amy Blankson, author of *The Future of Happiness*, cofounder of Digital Wellness Institute, and former member of the UN Global Happiness Council

"So important, so timely, so empowering, with tips that educate, enlighten, and empower us without shaming, scolding, or turning us into luddites."
—Dr. Christopher Willard, PsyD; lecturer in psychiatry at Harvard Medical School and author of twenty books, including *Growing Up Mindful* and *Alphabreaths*

"Based on lived experience, discernment, and community, this book offers us a path to integrating technology and AI into our lives without becoming overly determined by its pull. Over years, I have seen Jay Vidyarthi tracking and mapping our collective transition to transhumanism and—surprisingly—he remains hopeful. He is now ready to help us manage the technology we depend on. Hope for a better world comes in many forms—grab it wherever you can!"

—Michele Chaban, M/RSW, PhD; pioneer in applied mindfulness and palliative care, University of Toronto; and former clinical director, Mount Sinai Hospital (Toronto)

"You may have rolled your eyes at tech optimists arguing that tech will solve all our problems. You may have scoffed at hippies telling you to get a dumbphone. *Reclaim Your Mind* is the first book to propose a middle way. Jay shows you how to enjoy tech while maintaining your sanity. I couldn't stop sending quotes to my family and friends! *Reclaim Your Mind* is the first realistic and helpful theory and practice of tech wellbeing. It'll bring joy to your life and unlock your potential."

—Toby Sola, founder of the Brightmind Meditation app

Reclaim Your Mind

Reclaim Your Mind

*Seven Strategies to
Enjoy Tech Mindfully*

JAY VIDYARTHI

FOREWORD BY DANIEL J. SIEGEL, MD

Copyright © 2025 by Jay Vidyarthi

All rights reserved.

No part of this book may be reproduced, or stored in a retrieval system, or transmitted in any form or by any means, electronic, mechanical, photocopying, recording, or otherwise, without express written permission of the publisher.

Published by Still Ape Press, Kingston, Ontario
jayvidyarthi.com

Quotes from Tim Wu and Sebene Selassie reprinted with permission from the authors via personal correspondence.

Excerpt from *Zen Mind, Beginner's Mind* by Shunryu Suzuki © 1970. Reprinted by arrangement with Shambhala Publications, Inc., Boulder, CO.

Excerpt from *When Things Fall Apart: Heart Advice for Difficult Times by Pema Chödrön* © 2016. Reprinted by arrangement with Shambhala Publications, Inc., Boulder, CO.

Edited and designed by Girl Friday Productions
www.girlfridayproductions.com

Cover design: David Fassett
Project management: Kristin Duran
Editorial production: Kylee Hayes

ISBN (paperback): 978-1-0690995-0-1
ISBN (ebook): 978-1-0690995-1-8

First edition

To Indrakant and Oliver:

Only three generations apart, and a completely different way of life.

If we desire a future that avoids the enslavement of the propaganda state as well as the narcosis of the consumer and celebrity culture, we must first acknowledge the preciousness of our attention and resolve not to part with it as cheaply or unthinkingly as we so often have. And then we must act, individually and collectively, to make our attention our own again, and so reclaim ownership of the very experience of living.

—Tim Wu

CONTENTS

Foreword xvii
Introduction 1

PART ONE: ATTENTION ACTIVISM

1. The Attention Economy 17
2. Mindfulness as Activism 31
3. The Nature of Technology 47
4. A Day in the Digital Life 61

PART TWO: SEVEN STRATEGIES

5. Start with Awareness 75
6. See Through Conceptual Illusions 86
7. Fight Design with Design 99
8. Nurture Authenticity, Online and Off 112
9. Set Boundaries for Positive Ritual 123
10. Reject False Urgency 133
11. Vote for Better Tech 145

Conclusion 156

Acknowledgments 165
Glossary 167
References 171
Resources 177
About the Author 185

FOREWORD

BY DANIEL J. SIEGEL, MD
FOUNDER, WHOLE MIND CATALYST AND MINDSIGHT INSTITUTE

Jay Vidyarthi offers us a playful, wise, and practical guide to our modern challenge of how to relate to technology. With a background, personally and professionally, in exploring how to best connect with the ever-changing digital world, this insightful guide helps us approach technology with the mind's capacities for focused attention, open awareness, and relational connection in a realistic and helpful way.

The mind is both fully embodied and fully relational. Our mental lives emerge from energy flow that happens inside our body—including its brain and distributed nervous system—as well as between these bodies that we are born into, the world around us, the worlds of other people, and nature itself. This energy flow is not some nonscientific notion but a real, empirically validated aspect of the world in which we live.

It is this flow that captures our attention, fills our awareness in the moment, and draws us into relational connection. When we ask how technology influences us or how we can best use technology in our lives, we are essentially asking how to handle the increasing digital transformation of this energy flow into packets of on-off units of symbolic meaning. We call it "information," but you can think of it as *energy-in-a-formation* that stands for something, that symbolizes something more than light from a screen or sound from a speaker.

Many digital platforms seek to capture our attention and draw our energy into their complex webs of information flow. They are designed to capture "us"—to compel us to focus attention and fill awareness with their patterns over our own. This is our collective and individual challenge as we are then no longer voluntarily directing attention; instead, our attention is being captured beyond our control or even awareness. Without consciousness or intention, we expend the energy of our most vital resource—our minds.

Attention is both an essential skill and a fundamental nature of our minds. It involves the directing of energy flow and shaping how that flow is configured as information. Attention can be directed by us with intention, but increasingly often it is being pulled without our choice. This book aims to give you back that choice.

To be "mindful" has various research definitions, but broadly speaking, it involves two or three foundational components. One is the *focus of attention* determined by our own choice. A second is the *opening of awareness* so we are not swept up by objects of attention, enabling a "meta-awareness" of noticing what is in the field of awareness itself. A third component of "mindfulness" for many (but not all) researchers is kindness. We bring a positive regard, a loving approach—what I sometimes call a "COAL" state of mind, a mnemonic for curiosity, openness, acceptance, and love—to our moment-by-moment experience.

All three of these pillars serve as the essence of how and why Jay Vidyarthi guides us to intentionally shape our own mindful relationship with technology. Not only with strengthened attention and open awareness, but also with curiosity, openness, acceptance, and love.

With this valuable book, you will learn to have choice in the ways you enjoy technology by regulating how the energy flow of your attention and awareness are interfacing with this digital world. Jay's strategies provide a fun and effective way to gently strengthen your inner and relational mind to create more joy and more agency in your connection with technology.

For your own personal and professional life—and for your role as a parent, therapist, or coach—*Reclaim Your Mind* will benefit you now and help generations to come find a healthier way of living with strength in our technological world. Congratulations Jay, and congratulations to you for taking the time and energy to let this wise book guide your journey ahead.

INTRODUCTION

AT HOME IN TWO WORLDS

I love technology, and sometimes I love to get away from it.

As a kid in the eighties, I got excited about learning new magic words for the DOS command prompt. I remember that feeling of awe when I was able to code my own little games in BASIC. As I got older, I used early instant messengers like ICQ to flirt and hand-coded a Geocities website for no purpose other than to explore.

I waited way too long for images of my favorite anime characters to load, and even longer for MP3s to download. I spent countless hours waging epic ten-hour online battles that left my eyes feeling like hot coals. This was back when the only way to game online was to use a fax modem and a landline to trick PC games into thinking you were on a local area network. The lag was awful, but it worked.

If you're too young to recognize any of this software, I'm talking about the ancestors of modern digital life. So, yeah, I'm pretty techy. But I also grew up with deep exposure to yoga and meditation, since my parents immigrated to Canada from India. I saw my father meditate often, and my mother worships Hindu deities, like Hanuman, the monkey god who tried to eat the sun.

I visited Hindu temples and experienced many of the rites and rituals. Meditation and yoga felt more like a part of my heritage than esoteric practices. But let's be real, it was something my parents did, so at best I ignored it. At worst I did what most teenagers do: I rolled my eyes.

As I came of age, tech became my love language. My well-earned digital flirting expertise was clutch when I met Krista, the woman who would eventually become my wife. We were guarded in person, but had long, deep conversations in text. We bonded over video games. By then, I played a lot less than I did when I was a kid, but I made up for the missing screen time at work.

I studied psychology and learned how to apply it to design. I was making tech easier to use, and the job had me swimming in emails, project management, and digital design tools. Spending all day on a screen, I came to find out that working on a computer wasn't all that different from video games. My career quickly became an RPG with dollars instead of experience points and real skills instead of equipment and magic.

The design work was exciting at first, but it got stale quick. Helping a business improve its conversion rate wasn't as fun as saving the world in *Final Fantasy*. Soon even my favorite tech hobbies started to feel meaningless. I slipped more and more into distraction. Work all day on a laptop, then come home to the warm glow of my TV, phone, and that same laptop.

I felt numb.

A search for meaning led me to some questionable choices, but it also led me back to meditation. It helped me feel less numb, even if only for a few minutes, but I didn't fully commit to making it a consistent part of my life. I was too busy.

For a while, my life was swinging like a pendulum between the dull comfort of modernity and the inward pursuit of something deeper. Over time, the split focus started to take its toll on me. I was spending all my personal time trying to cope with a stressful professional life that felt hollow.

Things started to change after I spent the better part of a year paying attention to my breath. It wasn't at a remote mountain retreat center amid the trees, as you might expect. My body was suspended in a tech research lab, where I was wearing biosensors, surrounded by loudspeakers. On paper, I was trying to get my graduate degree. What I was really doing was bringing distinct parts of myself together.

My thesis project involved designing, building, and publishing about an experimental technology for mindfulness called Sonic Cradle. It was a sensory deprivation chamber where participants composed layered music through breath work, and I meticulously designed it to sneak people into a state of mindfulness.

I meditated with Sonic Cradle for hours every day, occasionally pausing to tinker with the algorithm. Up until that point, I'd only dabbled with meditation. A research lab was a strange place for my first period of sustained practice, but it had a profound impact on me.

I found I could feel again, finally experiencing some of the emotional depth I usually ignored. I began to meditate more consistently and went on many silent retreats. I experimented with every style of meditation I could find, from evidence-based training programs to ancient traditional practices. Sonic Cradle wasn't just a springboard into a deeper personal meditation practice; it also ended up being the seed of a new career direction and lifestyle.

I left the university and joined a start-up where I helped design and launch Muse, a brain-sensing wearable device that gives the user neurofeedback during and after meditation. Sonic Cradle and Muse turned out to be the first two of about fifty mindful technologies I've helped create and improve over the years, many of which you can find in academic journals, app stores, and store shelves.

So here I am, at home in two worlds. I never picked a side. I'm still infinitely curious about every new app, gadget, and content drop. Yet I also love silent meditation retreats, long to spend time in monasteries, and try to stay in the present moment. As a parent, I celebrate my son Oliver's love of technology while coaching him to think and feel deeply and make good choices. In my professional life, I thrive at the intersection of mindfulness and technology.

Can I be a true meditator if I go home and play *Zelda*? Do I really fit in the tech world if I refuse to profit from things that distract, isolate, or divide us? Does occasionally staying up late to watch silly videos or an extra episode of TV make me less qualified to teach mindfulness? Are Krista and I failing as parents because we love playing video games with little Oliver?

Of course I grapple with these questions. But any time I try to abandon tech, I feel like I'm abandoning my very nature. And on the other hand, whenever I give in to tech fully, I feel mindless, distracted, and frustrated. I wrote this book because I've lived both ways and found neither to be wholly satisfying.

I'm fascinated by technology, yet I yearn for a calm, peaceful life. This dual interest led me to draw insights from both camps and experiment with a mindful way of being with technology, not against it. For my entire adult life, I've been trying to figure out how to live mindfully and love technology at the same time.

On my journey so far, I've found seven strategies that have helped me heal my relationship with technology and, ultimately, with myself. I think you might find them useful too. They will help you nurture a secure, guilt-free relationship with technology. I won't recommend you get rid of your phone, give up on knowledge work, or renounce social media. Instead, we'll explore practices and approaches that help you forge a healthier dialogue with technologies you intentionally choose to include in your life.

SWING LOW, SWEET PENDULUM

You might notice your own relationship with technology also swings between extremes, like a pendulum. Sometimes, you might be completely absorbed by technology—infinitely scrolling through apps, building your career online, scarfing down your meals in front of a screen, and cuddling with your smartphone at night.

When you hit your limit, the pendulum swings the other way. You either try to unplug and lock yourself out, or you continue with constant use, feeling distracted and unwell, riddled with guilt, shame, and regret. It can feel like you have no choice.

Once I tasted mindfulness on retreat, I started to get frustrated with living so much of my everyday life staring at screens. This led me to create all kinds of rules and systems for myself. I'd try to live a strict life of tech austerity. I'd delete my favorite apps. I'd aggressively forbid myself from watching any TV. I even got rid of our TV completely for a while.

It often felt like I was parenting my inner child: *If you keep watching so much TV, I'm gonna take it away!* It worked about as well as it does with my son: I'd eventually rebel and rebound into spending all my time in front of the TV. I'd take an exhausted walk of shame, heading to bed in the early hours of the morning, berating myself for wasting so much time. I'd binge-watch every night until I felt guilty enough to ban myself from TV again. And the cycle would continue, rinsing and repeating all the way to burnout.

I got angry when I realized this wasn't a coincidence. Tech designers (like me) are mostly paid to tweak digital products for maximum engagement. It's our job to make small design changes to trick the mind and keep users hooked on the app, game, or feed. No wonder I couldn't find balance with it!

Mindfulness was a lifeline, but I still loved tech and found it useful and rewarding in so many ways. I ended up spending the next decade bringing awareness to my own relationship to technology. I knew there had to be a way to be present and balanced while enjoying and working in tech. It had to be possible.

As I experimented with tools and strategies, it eventually became clear that the problem wasn't so much with the extremes—it was the constant feeling of dissatisfaction. I felt guilty for using too much tech, and a bored FOMO when I disconnected. It felt like something was wrong all the time.

The first step was to stop resisting the way things are. I needed to embrace my patterns—and the modern world that created them. A part of me loves technology, and a part of me is frustrated by it. Both are true. I love a quiet moment, but sometimes it gets boring and I want to play a video game. It's all good. Life moves in cycles, and that's okay.

Everything changed when I accepted the pendulum and let it swing.

In mindfulness meditation, we learn not to strive for perpetual calm, relaxation, or boundless love. Instead, we learn to accept the movements of the mind and relate to them in a healthy way. I rolled my eyes at this stuff as a kid, but now I finally see that my ancestors taught a method to find balance with whatever we're experiencing, feeling, or thinking about. As it turns out, this level of awareness is essential in navigating and establishing a mindful relationship with technology too.

I've learned to find equilibrium and ignore those who declare one extreme superior to the other. I've learned to let go of the guilt-trip and ignore advice that tries to shame me for being fascinated by tech. Instead, I notice, understand, and tweak my own natural cycles. This has led me to healthier habits, and more importantly, I've learned how to enjoy tech without getting stuck on it.

I do watch TV, play games, use social media, work remotely, and stay up to date with the news. I have a busy email inbox and shared calendar organizing my work. I do these things with intention, and I find lots of joy and connection from all of it.

I rarely find myself mindlessly going down the internet rabbit hole anymore. When I do, I accept it as a part of my pendulum's swing and enjoy the release. If it happens too often, I'm able to skillfully and gently redirect my pendulum without beating myself up about it.

I don't believe techno-optimists who say we should dive completely into the metaverse, accelerating to the singularity. Nor do I buy into wellness influencers who want to opt out of modern life and switch to dumbphones. Neither extreme has worked or will ever work for me—and I know I'm not the only one.

There is a middle ground. A lot of tech is problematic, but we can enjoy the benefits if we learn to see clearly and use wisely. Still, finding that balance is not easy. Tech is infinitely compelling and can suck a lot of our time and energy.

Drawing clear boundaries is essential. To fall in love with the best of tech all over again, we must first reclaim our minds from the worst of it. Yet we limit ourselves not because we think technology is bad but because we want it to serve us better.

Don't let a few bad apps ruin the bunch. Just because fire can burn down your house doesn't mean you stop using it to cook your food, right? Peace will not come from fighting your natural cycles of connection and disconnection; it will come from dropping the resistance and integrating the wisdom of both extremes.

There's no need to chastise ourselves for excessive technology use, nor to abandon modernity in pursuit of some idealized vision of a free-range, wandering life (especially if that's not what you actually want). It's okay to enjoy what works for you while boycotting what exploits you.

So let the pendulum swing. Accept it. From there, let's work together to skillfully alter its trajectory to fit the life you truly want to lead.

WHAT TO EXPECT FROM THIS BOOK

As technology has woven itself ever deeper into our lives, some wellness influencers have started to advocate for digital balance, but it somehow never quite feels like they're speaking to people who enjoy tech the way I do. They tend to talk about it as a nuisance. A necessary evil. They recommend we merely tolerate it because we have to, but other than that, they tell us to disconnect whenever possible. It's a reasonable stance, as some of our technology can seem quite harmful, and a lot of it is entangled in systems that don't have our best interests at heart.

On the other end of the spectrum, much of mainstream society remains blissfully oblivious, diving headfirst into the digital abyss, with sophisticated gadgets moving into more and more intimate parts of life. We crave online validation, hunt for constant stimulation, and too easily give up on the physical world. Once in a while, we look up from our screens only to feel understimulated, lonely, numb, and aimless.

This book is a call to action for those who, like me, want to move from a love-hate relationship with technology to a mindful one. It will empower you to reclaim your attention and take back your technology, rather than letting both be hijacked. It's for those who believe it's possible to enjoy digital entertainment, keep up with the latest, and stay connected to work in a free and balanced way.

But you're tired. I get it. Before we pour effort into making changes, we'll reframe how you think about tech at the root level. We'll plant seeds that naturally flower into changes in the moment. Sometimes awareness is enough.

In Part One: Attention Activism, we'll lay the

groundwork. I'll cover how the modern economy is designed to harvest attention and why mindfulness has become a critical form of resistance. I'll tell some personal stories of how I got here and what a mindful relationship with tech could look like for you. Part One will help you reframe things in a way that leads to effortless changes in your life. Knowing is half the battle.

In Part Two: Seven Strategies, we'll get much more practical. We'll use familiar examples to explore my list of tried-and-true strategies you can use to enjoy tech mindfully. I'll guide you in how to engage with technologies that can be truly fun and useful while identifying and boycotting those that can be problematic for you personally. We'll cover TV, movies, texting, work email, social media, gaming, AI, and more. At the end, we'll even explore technologies designed explicitly to help you be more mindful, many of which my peers and I helped create. Pro tip: the chapter titles in Part Two might be worth putting up on your wall.

While Part Two is the fun part, where you'll get to try stuff to mindfully transform your relationship with technology, I recommend devoting some quality time to Part One. When you know why tech is the way it is and why you relate to it in the way you do, it will become much easier to make lasting changes and stick to new habits.

Before we get into it, I also want to make a quick note about what this book is *not*. While I will discuss mindfulness at length, this is not a how-to meditation guide. I won't tell you how to sit in any specific posture, how to breathe, or how long to practice. There are plenty of other places you can get that information, and I've included a few of my favorites in the Resources section at the end of the book.

Still, direct experience is a great teacher, so each chapter concludes with a lightweight hands-on activity to help you get a feel for the material, though I've specifically designed them to not require any background in meditation.

It's also important to mention that this book is not a replacement for mental health care. Tech is so powerful and omnipresent that it can exacerbate and potentially even cause depression, anxiety, and self-harm. Especially for young people, life online can be disturbing, destabilizing, and disheartening. It's rare, but some people even find themselves with medical-grade addictions to social media, video games, or pornography.

If you're under sixteen, there are unique aspects of social, cultural, and brain development that may make tech especially problematic for you. Even as you get into your early twenties, you might still find some of the ideas here harder to implement, as your brain hasn't yet reached its full capacity for self-regulation. The same could be true if you're neurodivergent in ways that affect executive function.

I am writing to mitigate harm, provide support, and help rekindle the joy of tech in a way that's relevant for as many people as possible. But that doesn't mean my approach will work the same way for everyone or that you should go it alone. There are lots of professionals who specialize in mental health, childhood development, and neurodiversity, and you might be surprised by how supportive they can be.

We've only scratched the surface, but as you can probably already tell, your relationship with tech is complex and multifaceted. Like any relationship, you clash at times. Later you might fall in love all over again. Your tech might lead you to transformation or to burnout. It might introduce you to lifelong friends, but it might also lead to awful miscommunications and toxic social dynamics. Tech can be so fun and so fascinating, yet it can also be so frustrating and fragmenting. Relationships take work. Sometimes you might need some time apart.

All these experiences are valid. Tech has its strengths and weaknesses. There are positives and negatives. The human tendency to polarize everything is not serving us. We love to think in terms of good and evil. When ChatGPT was released, the world got its first taste of new breakthroughs in artificial intelligence. It instantly sparked two competing visions of the future: either we were going to be served by the *Star Trek* computer and the Jetsons' robot maid, or we'd end up with Terminators and Death Stars.

Our actual future lies between these extremes. And so does our present. Technology is neither enemy nor friend; it's a fun-house mirror reflecting and distorting our societal and personal values. If we're serious about maintaining sanity while society accelerates, finding authenticity in our own personal relationships with technology is one of the most important things we can do.

TRY: MINDFUL READING

Let's try a sixty-second exercise exploring what it's like to be mindful while engaged with visual information. No need to close your eyes or sit in any special way; just read on and see what happens.

Step 1: Slow down your reading pace right now. Keep reading these words, but gradually slow down. Take a breath. Even slower. Maybe . . . one . . . word . . . every . . . second.

Step 2: Listen to your inner voice. If you pay close attention, you can hear your inner voice saying each word. Listen to how it sounds in your mind.

Step 3: Notice the visual experience of reading. As you continue listening to that inner voice, notice how your visual focus moves from word to word. Be aware of how your eye jumps across the text, scanning across the words.

Step 4: Keep it slow. If you notice yourself speeding up, slow . . . down . . . again. Read each word deliberately. Sound out each syllable in your mind. Notice the shape of each word and the space between.

Step 5: Gradually accelerate back to normal reading. Let all these instructions evaporate as you slowly step back into reading in a natural way.

Step 6: Pause to reflect. What was it like to meditate while reading? How did it feel to slow down and pay attention to each word? How was this different from how you normally read? Did you notice any new insights or perspectives?

PART ONE

ATTENTION ACTIVISM

1

THE ATTENTION ECONOMY

Human beings are so desperate for attention that the most successful technologies are the ones that tell us that other people are paying attention to us, that we matter, and that we're loved. It's not a coincidence. Designers and marketers are trained to hook us by hacking into our emotional needs and perceptual systems. It works.

Growing up, I was lucky. I had two parents who loved me and did their best. Still, it wasn't always easy for me to get attention. My mother had some mental health challenges to deal with, so she wasn't always present in the moment. My father had his hands full providing for us. Like with many fathers of his generation, the best way to get his attention was through competition, achievement, and success.

My older brother and I had a good connection, but there was a lot of sibling rivalry too. At school, he was this charismatic overachiever who was damn good at everything he tried. I was constantly trying to figure out how to live in his shadow. I couldn't quite impress my dad or anyone at school the way my brother could. I had a difficult time getting anyone to pay attention to me. This all added up to me desperately craving attention from the outside world for decades.

In elementary school, I made a lot of trouble. I was in the office frequently for acting up. I remember one specific day when I got sent to the office for beating up a kid named Geoff. He and a few others played a prank that had them secretly agreeing to avoid me at recess. Having no one pay attention to me hurt so much that I totally lost it. Unfortunately for Geoff, he was the slowest in the pack. Sorry, Geoff.

During high school, I followed my brother's lead and realized there were better ways to get attention. I wanted to be popular. I made acquaintanceships with everyone at the expense of actual friendships. I'd go to school dances hoping to impress everyone with my skills. I joined theater productions, became student council president, and eventually gave the valedictory address by popular vote. I got good grades—mostly to get a pat on the head. I'd do anything to get people to notice me.

By age twenty, I started drinking a lot and loved acting the fool at parties. It was an even easier way to get attention. Soon after that, I realized that nothing commanded the room's attention like controversy and conflict, so I talked a lot of shit with strangers and felt an incredible rush when my friends and I ended up in drunken brawls in front of everyone.

Seeing the pattern yet? The story continues.

Music became a private outlet for me at home, but when I first performed at an open mic, I tasted another rush of attention and got hooked. When first building my professional design career, I especially loved presenting work, giving talks, and finding other ways to be seen and heard. I published articles and relished any positive feedback I'd get from bosses, clients, colleagues, and users.

So much good has come from this journey, but there has been a subtle anxiety underlying it all. So many of my choices as a child, teenager, and young man were driven by an insatiable need for attention. I hated being ignored and became hypervigilant about how I was perceived. Despite good outcomes, I now recognize my unhealthy fixation on getting a form of love so many of us crave: attention.

It wasn't a coincidence that as I grew up and got less praise from parents, teachers, and audiences, I started to feel lost and numb. I wasn't taking any courses, it wasn't cool to get too drunk anymore, and our band hadn't taken off the way we'd hoped.

Without a source of positive attention from other people, I became pretty dissatisfied with life. I craved for people to like me, to see me, to be impressed by me. How fragile I was. I didn't notice at the time, but this desperate need for attention was failing to give me any true sense of meaning or purpose.

I know I'm not alone in this. I see it online every day. Social media, games, work email, news, dating apps, and so on: they all provide us with so much productivity, fun, information, and connection. Yet we can also find ourselves compulsively using them in futile attempts to fill the holes in our hearts.

In this chapter, I'll introduce you to how new technologies harvest our attention and shift the way we experience life. At this point, it's more about seeing clearly than changing anything. The first step is to see the world for what it is.

THE CURRENCY OF WAKING LIFE

We live in a system in which human attention is a commodity being bought and sold—experts call it the **attention economy**. The winners of our society are those who can capture and organize information in ways that are impossible to ignore. Most of the largest companies in the world succeed by harvesting our attention and selling it to the highest bidder.

Social media companies create wealth by collecting data about you and using it to drive targeted advertising. E-commerce giants, messaging platforms, and streaming services profit from using similar data profiles to deliver smart recommendations and irresistible in-app purchases. In our largest organizations, we work on understanding people to better exploit them for profit.

This isn't new. In June 1836, French newspaper *La Presse* had a novel idea—charge businesses to put messages in their weekday edition. They were among the first to discover the value of selling the attention of their captive readership. In other words, advertising.

Not too long after that, traveling salesmen were selling literal snake oil, nation-states were using catchy slogans to recruit soldiers, and a manipulative marketing campaign snuck cigarettes into the suffragette movement to get the world smoking.

In the late nineteenth and early twentieth centuries, advertising took off as a major industry. This was the root of an economy that values attention as a commodity. Now, tech companies, news media, political parties, businesses, digital creators, and more all fight to get our attention. What's strange is that we freely give it to them without a second thought. Gold is valuable on the market, yet we also think of it as precious in our personal lives. But when it comes to our attention, we just give it away.

When I started meditating, I stopped giving it away so easily. I realized that attention is the priceless currency of my waking life—and let's face it: our time here is limited. What we pay attention to defines our experience of living. When I started to see how much of a role attention played in my overall well-being, I decided to stop letting it be constantly stolen without my consent.

Sometimes we don't even realize the digital sleight of hand these apps pull to maximize our screen time at all costs. Professional designers like me are choreographers of attention. This isn't necessarily a bad thing: we made stop signs bright red to capture your attention while you're driving and remind you to stop at an intersection. Yet we also create sophisticated digital platforms that profit from harvesting hours of your attention per day.

We've built a vast empire of tools online to placate our deepest emotional needs with simple illusions. Comments are not conversations. Views don't often help us feel truly seen. No digital heart or thumbs-up gives us the love we need. We think we're putting ourselves out there for all to see when really we're projecting an image. Most will scroll by, barely registering that we exist.

We cherish metrics that mean nothing more than a stranger spending a few seconds with our words and images on their screen. If we don't get enough, we try to change who we are to satisfy the algorithm—which is constantly shifting and impossible to pin down. But what about *our* satisfaction? Wasn't the whole point of all this tech to increase our quality of life and solve our problems?

Instead we get a temporary hit while the platforms profit. Ironically, a lot of that money goes to people climbing the corporate ladder because they're desperate for attention too.

Individuals and organizations all want attention so badly that we've built a whole economy around it. Yet instead of helping us feel loved and accepted for who we are, we're finding ourselves distracted and polarized. We hide behind our devices and pretend to be someone we think people will love because we don't believe anyone could love us for who we really are.

TECHNOLOGY AND MENTAL HEALTH

Inspired by my work as a designer, my growing mindfulness practice, and Sherry Turkle's heartfelt intuition in *Alone Together*, I started writing about these issues in the summer of 2016. Even my wife, Krista, looked at me like I was wearing a tinfoil hat and spouting conspiracy theories. Many others felt defensive. At the time, the general public was still in tech's honeymoon period, and no one wanted to hear that these incredible, cherished devices could be problematic.

I found early kinship in the work of Tristan Harris, a former Google employee who started publicly calling for tech companies to respect users' time in a movement he called Time Well Spent. His work eventually evolved into the Center for Humane Technology, a nonprofit that has been engaged in advocacy work with business and government leaders. They also produced *The Social Dilemma*, an illuminating yet ominous documentary summarizing the issues with social media.

Tim Wu's *The Attention Merchants* gave me the history, and James Williams's *Stand Out of Our Light* philosophically positioned this movement to be about freedom, but it wasn't until I found the work of Jean Twenge that I truly felt my instincts were starting to be validated. A psychologist by training, Twenge published a book called *iGen*, which summarized a massive dataset showing dramatic differences between Gen Z and previous generations. A number of those findings pertain to mental health, social changes, and developmental delays. At the time, Twenge was relying on large-scale surveys, and she only had enough data to *correlate* technology with these concerning trends.

More recently, another psychologist and author, Jonathan Haidt, collaborated with Twenge to summarize the growing evidence and make a stronger case that tech is playing a significant role in actively *causing* a collapse in mental health for young people in *The Anxious Generation*. The book draws causality between what Haidt calls the "phone-based childhood" and anxiety, depression, self-harm, and suicide. It also associates social media with eating disorders, bullying, and collapses in self-esteem for young girls. Boys seem to be affected less by social media, but they make up for it with their own set of potential problems relating to video games, pornography, and addiction.

As a parent myself, I know well the panic that comes from seeing how these issues might threaten our kids. Some experts, like Dr. Andrew Przybylski at Oxford and

Dr. Pete Etchells in his book *Unlocked*, don't yet see enough evidence to draw causality or take immediate action. Still, many are already calling for regulation, and some schools are already putting bans in place. Time will reveal how these restrictions impact actual behavior and outcomes.

Much of the research focuses on young people and mental health (for good reason), but *all of us* are being affected by technology. It will take time for experts to sort out how it impacts diverse people and communities. The issue takes a classic political shape—it pits individual freedom against collective regulation in context of a multitrillion-dollar industry—so it will take even longer for regulators and changemakers to find consensus on if and how to intervene.

In the meantime, you are not helpless.

As an individual, you don't need to wait for academic certainty, regulation, more ethical corporations, or a mental health diagnosis. What if you paid closer attention to how you relate to different technologies? Are you able to see directly what's serving you and what's exploiting you? You don't need anyone's permission to make intentional choices about which technologies to give up and which ones to enjoy. You just need clarity of motivation and effective strategies. We have a lot of work to do in our organizations, but there is also much you can do in your individual life, and if you have kids, teach them to do the same.

In only a decade, we've transitioned from blissful ignorance to widespread concern around tech's problems with privacy, mental health, inequity, public discourse, and more. While the original ad-based social media model might eventually fade, the attention economy is here to stay. The genie is out of the bottle. People and organizations know they can profit and gain power when they use sophisticated tech to capture attention en masse. This isn't going to change anytime soon. The next wave of AI-driven platforms is only going to strengthen and multiply the ways we can manipulate each other. Are you going to let that wave bowl you over, stealing your precious attention and time, or will you be ready?

SUBTLE INFLUENCE IS POWERFUL

There's a lot of science fiction about sentient artificial intelligence rising up to destroy its human creators. We've long been imagining tech outpacing us and deciding to squash or enslave us, from Skynet to HAL 9000 to Cylons to Agent Smith. But people using AI over the past decade have shown future robot rebellions a more efficient path to domination: getting us to destroy ourselves by subtly influencing how we think, feel, and behave.

In early civilizations, it must have seemed perfectly okay to let a shopkeeper influence potential customers by posting a message in the town square, especially since anyone could easily choose to ignore or engage with it. With time, even just making that message a little catchy and placing it in a high-traffic area would have seemed fairly reasonable.

In the information age, things have changed. Ads are now sophisticated messages that systematically target your desires, insecurities, and fears. Each tactic is often only one part of an almost militaristic campaign to command your attention and trigger a change in behavior.

Political parties motivate us with fear. Corporations

make us feel like we're missing something. Products are strategically placed in TV shows. The media disguise paid ads as unbiased journalism. Even cash-strapped schools sell ad space in their cafeterias.

Tech platforms collect data about us at every turn and build digital profiles of who we are. They use this information to target our feeds, search results, and recommendations. When an advertiser knows everything about you, it takes a lot of effort to resist. Especially when paid messages ping the devices in your pocket and on your bedside table.

The machine-learning techniques that helped create this state of affairs are rudimentary compared to today's AI. Yet they still played a significant role in influencing elections, reducing our attention spans, and raising mental health debates. As we enter a new era of much more powerful intelligent systems, the battle for human attention will wage on.

Putting a poster up in the town square feels quite different from an artificial intelligence trained to collect and use your intimate data. Does it violate some fundamental human right to be subjected to big-budget operations with the explicit goal of subtle influence? At least we can agree that it goes beyond the term "marketing." It might be better described as manipulation, propaganda, or even *Inception*.

Sophisticated generative AIs have landed in a world where large organizations harvest and trade attention for power, prestige, and profit. As we get better at manipulating each other, there's no reason to believe well-being or quality of life will take priority.

There are connected devices in our pockets, on our wrists, and in our glasses. There are screens in our bedrooms, offices, pubs, public transportation, and waiting rooms. On those screens are ideas scaled so fast that their consequences are impossible to predict. It's easy to feel helpless when large forces are so deeply incentivized to harvest our minds. We're stuck on our roofs in a rising flood of information.

If your first instinct is to retreat, I can relate.

OPTING OUT OF THE ATTENTION ECONOMY

It's dead winter in Montreal. I'm in a giant unfinished basement space with only one industrial heater in the corner of the room. I can see my breath. I'm with four guys and we're all in winter jackets, feverishly playing drums, keyboards, and guitars to keep warm.

Our band fell apart a year ago, shattering our wannabe rock star egos. It's clear the music isn't going to get everyone to love and pay attention to me the way I'd hoped. We're jamming together one last time before we lose access to our rehearsal space.

We were a bit rusty at first, but now we're getting into the zone. Drums in the pocket with an arpeggiated synth. Hypnotizingly repetitive bass lines and guitar licks. Free vocal exploration on the mics.

That day, we weren't trying to write a hit song. That dream was dead. Instead, we freely jammed continuously for almost an hour. As the jam ended, I basked in the silence, and I felt different.

I was buzzing. I put my guitar back on the stand with an epic level of clarity, seeing my hand anew, watching the colored lights reflect on the guitar strings. I could see differently. I was more focused. It felt like a glimpse into what I'd been missing in my life. Instead of craving the attention of others, I was directly accessing the raw power of my own attention for the first time.

I immediately connected this state of mind to the ancient practices my parents introduced to me. I knew very little about meditation and yoga at this point, but I knew they promised the ability to shift one's state of mind. Here I was experiencing blissful clarity from intense concentration. Could this be what the teachings were about?

It was in that moment that a path opened up to me that would change my personal and professional life. I started by researching Nada Yoga, a spiritual practice rooted in sound and music. Then I took a course in Hinduism and Buddhism, where I watched *Doing Time, Doing Vipassana*, a documentary about a ten-day silent meditation retreat in a high-security prison. Seeing hardened criminals repent for their crimes with tears streaming down their faces, I was mystified. I couldn't stop talking about it, but it was people close to me who actually found a nearby meditation center and signed up. When they came back transformed, I knew it was time to stop talking. I went online and booked my own ten-day silent retreat.

It didn't solve all my problems, but I did finally see how my need for others to pay attention to me had dominated my life. I learned to pay attention to myself instead. What if I could offer myself the love I was so desperately searching for? I tried to stick with the practice, but the momentum of modern life kept sucking me back into the same old patterns. I went on many more retreats to refresh my practice and found my rhythm over time.

In the midst of burnout, silent retreats felt like the only

source of meaning I had left. They were hard, but at least I felt something. Every time I went on a retreat or recommitted to the present moment, I felt the raw power of awareness. But it always slipped away again when I came back to everyday life. I learned vital skills to cope with and free myself from broken habits, but I was still overwhelmed. The pendulum continued to swing from extreme to extreme. It was exhausting.

I'd learned to recognize the attention economy and even to opt out for short periods of time, but I hadn't found balance. Something needed to change.

TRY: NOT TRYING

These days, one of the most radical things you can do is nothing at all. Simple, but not easy. Read through these instructions first, then put the book down and give it a try.

Step 1: Find a comfortable position. Find a way to relax, either sitting or lying down. Let your body settle in and set an intention to let go of all the effort for a while. Set a timer for at least a few minutes if you'd like.

Step 2: Let go of expectations. Take a few deep breaths to release any tension and let go of whatever came before this moment. Close your eyes if that helps you relax. Release any expectation you might be holding for this experience. Let whatever happen.

Step 3: Don't do anything. Shift from the mindset of trying to meditate or trying to relax or even trying to follow this exercise. Instead, don't try at all. Be with whatever arises. No need to change anything about what you're experiencing, just notice it.

Step 4: Radically accept your experience. Release any resistance to whatever comes up. If a thought arises, great, let it happen. If you naturally want to focus on your breath, great, let it happen. For this brief moment, whatever you're experiencing is okay exactly as it is.

Step 5: Stop trying. If you find yourself trying to control anything, just drop that effort. You don't need to fix anything, or try to make the most of this, or try to do it right. Let go of any pressure to achieve or accomplish.

Step 6: Carry this forward. Once your timer goes off or you decide to move on, reflect on how that felt. See if you can carry a sense of ease and okayness as you step back into doing.

2

MINDFULNESS AS ACTIVISM

By the end of 2017, I burnt out trying to forcefully cultivate inner peace while also drowning in screens and expectations. Thankfully, my wife was on a similar burnout trajectory, so at least I wasn't alone.

We were on the same page, totally disengaged from work, the fast pace of city life in Toronto, and all that stimulation. Every night we came home and stared at our devices, isolated in our tiny condo with a view of other condos. I scanned news headlines, watched videos, and compulsively glanced at work email and social media. Whenever I tried to meditate, I quickly drowned in thoughts and gave up.

A friend was getting married across the pond, so we took the opportunity to visit Scotland's Isle of Skye—easily one of the most beautiful places I will ever see. After hours of hiking the Hebridean coast (not a screen in sight), we tended the fire in our cabin with glasses of scotch. I felt true serenity wash over me, and my wife asked a loaded question point blank: "What the fuck are we doing in Toronto?"

I've always loved the big city, but staring over the rolling highland hills, it felt like a really good question. Life at home was so frantic. We were burning out on jobs that didn't fill our cups, only to come home glued to our screens, immersing ourselves in mindless entertainment, twenty-four-hour news cycles, and constant self-criticism. In an ambitious culture coupled with a high cost of living, it didn't feel like we had any control over our lives.

In retrospect, that was the moment we decided to be victims.

We blamed everything around us and tried to escape. We blamed calendar Tetris and Inbox Zero. We blamed streaming video, video games, and news feeds. We blamed big corporations, the city, and the economy. Blame, blame, blame. We thought if we could just get away from it all, we'd be happy. It didn't feel like a ten-day retreat would be enough this time. We quit our jobs, gave up our apartment, and left.

SO WHAT?

Our first stop was a monastery. We locked our phones away and moved in with the monastic community, ready for a more permanent retreat. It seemed like a good place to get some answers to questions that had long been swirling inside.

How do we live with clarity in the midst of all this hustle?

How do we find meaning when everything is all about money?

Is authenticity even possible when we're drowning in information?

Where should we live?

What should we do?

How should we be?

Ironically, deep meditation revealed that I didn't need answers to these questions. In fact, it was my compulsive need for answers itself that was holding me back. I was trying to conceptually understand everything. It was such a relief to stop obsessing over what our next step should be and instead just be okay with not knowing.

In my experience with silent retreats, you're usually meditating ten hours a day or more. Some days are brutally boring and frustrating, even painful. Other days feel more like climbing a mountain: it's difficult but rewarding to face the challenge. Most days are punctuated with moments of excruciating discomfort and, if you're sticking to the practice, moments of blissful inner peace too.

You wake up before the sun rises and stumble into the meditation hall for morning practice. From there, you follow a rigorous schedule of meditation surrounded by beautiful scenery. Even exercise, work, and meal breaks are done in silence, with the intention that you move and eat mindfully. You'd be surprised the level of clarity you can get on your own ego while cleaning a public toilet, mindfully listening to your inner voice explain how unfair it is and claiming that you're somehow above the task.

I'd been on many silent retreats at this point, yet I'd never had a day that felt easy until about five or six weeks into this particular one. It felt so calm and peaceful, which hadn't been the norm for me at all. That day, it was so easy to focus. Every meditation technique I tried worked wonders. It felt amazing.

At the end of the day, I had a practice interview with the head teacher, an abbot named Soryu Forall. I was excited to share my breakthrough with him. After listening, he paused for a moment, then his reply shocked me.

"So what?"

I was so proud of my achievement, and I really wanted a pat on the back. Instead, I was met with total dismissal.

At first, I felt hurt. Then I investigated that feeling. Wait, where is this hurt coming from? Why do I want his approval so badly? Oh, god. I wanted him to praise me the same way I always wanted it from my parents, teachers, bosses, and audiences. Even on a mountain in the middle of nowhere, weeks into a meditation retreat, I was still so desperate for approval. How did he know?

Over time, the wisdom of his prompt sank in. What at first felt like total dismissal was actually an incredibly compassionate thing to say to me in that exact moment. Why meditate? Why practice? Sure, I might get better at it, but what good does that do for anybody? What congratulations do I deserve for having a day of inner peace and mental clarity?

All of a sudden, disconnecting from the modern world to preserve my own mind felt pointless. Sure, I escaped the attention economy and found a remote hideout from the precarious state of the world. I meditated until my mind finally calmed down and settled into the present moment.

So what?

In as little as two words, he helped me see that a monastic retreat on a beautiful mountain could be just as empty as a life staring at screens in the big city if I didn't stay connected to a deeper sense of purpose. For some, that purpose might be to stay in the monastery and become a monk. We considered that, but I wasn't ready to give up on modern life. I felt called to continue my practice face-to-face with the attention economy.

I decided I couldn't blame my struggles on technology or the city anymore. This is not to say these things don't need to be continuously improved. They do. But I no longer felt like a victim. In our former lifestyle, my wife and I had simply lost track of the things that truly mattered. I wanted to try again, this time embracing the mystery and letting go of the need to figure everything out.

What would the attention economy feel like if I stayed connected to awareness? How would modern life treat me if I maxed out my sense of purpose and ruthlessly prioritized it above the need to get attention through power, prestige, or wealth? The learning had just begun.

The next day, I powered up my smartphone. A few days later, we were back on the road. A month later, my wife was pregnant. Later that year, I started my own business exclusively designing products for well-being, unapologetically shifting my career focus back to the intersection of mindfulness and technology.

Over time, I found out that the opposite of what I learned at the monastery was also true. A modern digital life full of aspirations, smartphones, and TV screens can be just as meaningful and natural as a quiet, contemplative life. Awareness is the key. In this chapter, we'll explore how mindfulness can help us take more agency in how we interface with the attention economy.

ATTENTION, AWARENESS, AND MINDFULNESS

You're paying attention to this book right now. Or maybe you're distracted, paying attention to something else while your eyes habitually move across the page. Let me try something: *fuck*. I bet that snapped your attention back to the page! Our names have the same kind of power. When someone says your name in a crowded space, you can't help but notice. A lot of technologies have this power too.

Attention is a fundamental capacity of your mind. Scientific experts on attention, like Dr. Gloria Mark, think of it as your ability to be conscious of some things while excluding other things. Sometimes we focus on one thing, other times our attention jumps all over the place. Sometimes we get distracted, sometimes we don't. These are all natural qualities of how attention moves over time.

Attention is something you can control only partially. The way you're paying attention to this book right now is an example of voluntary attention, where you choose intentionally to direct your mind. But as you know, you don't always have perfect control of this. Sometimes attention is involuntary.

If I've done my job well, this book will hold your attention for at least a little while. But it's still just a book. No matter how hard you try to focus on what you're reading, your attention will eventually wander off. According to work from Dr. Amishi Jha—a renowned neuroscientist who specializes in attention—things that are self-referential, unexpected, exciting, or threatening tend to be more effective at drawing your attention. It's hard to ignore a sudden bolt of lightning, a strange sound in your home when you're alone, or your ringtone.

We don't *only* experience this narrow vector we call attention. It takes place within a larger field of mysterious possibility: awareness. This is how you know when your phone rings even when you're not paying direct attention to it.

Awareness is an innate ability and a fundamental capacity of your mind. It isn't somewhere out there. It's not something you have to find or get. You are born with a wider general awareness of your mind, body, and world, and within that field, you pay attention in specific directions.

In every moment, what we experience is a dynamic interaction between attention and awareness. You may be narrowing your attention to this book right now, barely noticing anything else. If I cue you, you can continue reading while becoming more aware of what's around you. For example, as you read this sentence, listen to whatever sounds may be around you in your environment. Do you hear ambient noises like the air conditioning or the dryer running? Is there a barking dog outside or someone moving around in the next room? You've been peripherally aware of these sounds—along with body sensations and thoughts—but notice how you didn't really process them until you pointed your attention toward them.

A skilled mindfulness teacher can guide you even further. You can learn to observe this dynamic flow of experience without getting stuck. You watch the quality of attention as it narrows and broadens. You track attention as it flickers between thoughts, feelings, and sensations. You practice allowing these thoughts, feelings, and sensations to come and go without pushing or pulling.

The word "meditation" refers to a broad category of

practices. Many styles promote a state of mindfulness, which often means that they encourage you to gently notice what you're paying attention to, while you're paying attention to it. Scientists refer to this as meta-awareness.

The most important thing to know about meta-awareness is that it's a skill. The more we practice it, the more we're able to concentrate and see clearly. Over time, a heightened awareness seeps into the corners and cracks of daily life.

CHANGING YOUR DEFAULT MODE

Some people spend their whole lives practicing one style of meditation. Others wander and incorporate different approaches. I'm not married to any particular style, but when I find a technique that resonates, I tend to commit for a season or two. Different approaches have served me in different phases of life.

These days, I start by taking stock of what's happening in my body, mind, and the world around me, and I let that guide the tools and techniques I use from a growing repertoire. And sometimes, I know what I really need is to let go of any strategy and just be. Over time, I have learned to trust myself to know what I need in the moment.

Meditation is not one-size-fits-all. When you come in contact with different traditions and techniques, it's important to understand that people are diverse. We each bring unique lifestyles, perspectives, and histories to the practice. What works for one may not work for another. There are a lot of different paths up the mountain, and mysteriously enough, some are better off not trying too hard to climb any mountains.

My early explorations into Nada Yoga taught me to notice details I'd never noticed before through sound. My first silent retreat was in the Vipassana tradition of S. N. Goenka, the same style as the prisoners in that documentary I saw. It taught me how paying attention to my body—especially when I'm uncomfortable—could help me release repressed emotions and generate profound insight.

Since then, modern academic frameworks have taught me the importance of cultivating a nonjudgmental attitude and clear intention. Loving-kindness retreats with specific teachers and monks taught me how to take a gentler, loving approach. Classic literature helped me see these seemingly practical skills through a philosophical lens.

American meditation teacher Shinzen Young's *Five Ways to Know Yourself* taught me a language to communicate the subtleties of what I was experiencing. He provided a map I could use to chart my journey so far. I could pinpoint each of the different techniques I'd tried, and that helped me frame my experience. I could also clearly see the areas I hadn't yet explored, expanding my access to new techniques. I learned to be more responsive in my practice, adjusting my approach based on whatever happened in the moment.

This led me to the monastery where I trained with Soryu Forall, where he said "so what" and snapped me back to a sense of purpose. Soryu helped me directly experience a reality beyond my own rational mind. I painfully let go of the insatiable need to structure my knowledge and learned how awareness could be nonconceptual and direct, unfiltered by ideas. Experiencing this helped me let go of my craving for understanding.

When the COVID-19 pandemic hit, only one year after our son was born, my meditation practice fell apart. In an act of desperation, I began to practice in the only available window: while my wife was nursing during the bedtime routine. I was so exhausted that I couldn't bring much effort to the practice. For the first time, I saw the wisdom of the effortless way. I learned more about doing nothing, just sitting, and radical acceptance of the present moment.

Up until that point, most of my practice represented only one side of a spectrum of effort. I was always working, striving to get somewhere. Not trying so hard was healing, and since then I have learned to play with different levels of effort based on my needs in the moment. In fact, since then, playfulness has become a big part of my practice.

So far, this journey has not only improved my relationship with tech, it has led me to increased clarity, balance, and self-regulation. I'm better able to focus when I need to focus and relax when I want to relax. I find myself more resilient and better able to stay connected to a sense of purpose, especially when things get rough. I find myself more in touch with my emotions, less self-involved, and better able to enjoy and find fulfillment when things are going well.

And it's not just me.

Ever since 1979—when Jon Kabat-Zinn first created a clinical mindfulness program for use in hospitals—there has been a growing body of clinical and neuroscientific research on contemplative practices. Following up on great teachers who brought Eastern meditation to the West in the 1960s and 1970s, scientists have made huge strides in understanding what mindfulness is, how it works, and which of the many claimed benefits can be measured.

One of the most fascinating discoveries to come out of this research is a system of brain structures called the default-mode network. This network shows a flurry of activity when you're in your default mode: idling, waiting for the bus, daydreaming at work, ruminating, reflecting on yourself, and so on. When it seems like nothing much is going on around you, these specific areas of your brain are sending signals through trillions of synapses connecting billions of neurons in your default-mode network. No wonder it's so hard to stop thinking.

If someone is instructed to practice mindfulness in a brain scanner, we see the default-mode network power down. If we measure someone who's been meditating for an eight-week course or someone who's just come back from a one-month retreat, we'll see even less activation in the default-mode network. Someone who has been training in techniques that focus on attention and awareness for decades can make these specific brain regions go very quiet.

Now here's where it gets interesting. With experienced meditators, not only do we see much, much less activation in this network when they're meditating, they're also able to reduce activity at will when they're *not* meditating. They seem to have the ability to turn their default-mode network up and down like a volume knob. They can activate the thinking mind when they need it, and power it down when they don't. Waiting for the bus might feel very different for some people.

The neuroscience shows us that meditation strengthens attentional systems in the brain. It trains us to have more control over specific areas associated with mind wandering, creativity, and self-referential thinking. The more you practice, the stronger the effect. Best of all, these changes are associated with positive impacts on mental health and well-being.

There's evidence of meditation-based interventions reducing anxiety and depression and changing our relationship to pain, as well as indications of improvement in immune system function, better substance abuse outcomes, more resilience in challenging situations, better emotional regulation, enhanced productivity, increased autonomy, less ego involvement, and a whole lot more.

Dr. Richard Davidson and Dr. Daniel Goleman wrote the book on this, and their title sums it up well: *Altered Traits*. Training in mindfulness isn't only about feeling good while you meditate. In fact, it can get quite unpleasant, so if pleasure is your only motivation, you'll give up quick. We do it despite the challenge because it has the potential to make persistent changes to fundamental qualities of attention that define your life experience. In a way, it can change aspects of who you are.

For our purposes, I hope you see one thing clearly in all this. The growing body of scientific evidence confirms what I've experienced in my life and what many meditators have reported for thousands of years: mindfulness is a practice that can reliably help you regulate attention. And regulating attention is an essential part of what helps us thrive.

What could be more relevant in the attention economy?

ATTENTION ACTIVISTS, RISE UP!

If the science of mindfulness is new to you, this might feel like an exciting moment where meditation and academic research are colliding for the first time. I'm sorry to say that we're a bit late. This whole story goes way back.

For thousands of years, mystics explored mindfulness as part of countless traditions from all over the world. It was the baby boomers who translated Eastern practices and established them in the West. In the eighties, the Dalai Lama first met with scientists in Dharamshala, where they discussed the intersection between Western psychology and Buddhist philosophy, setting the stage for the scientific study of meditation. That might have been the real collision moment.

In the decades since, the science of mindfulness has grown in depth and breadth. The practice of meditation has become legitimized and more accessible in hospital rooms, boardrooms, classrooms, government offices, and more. It's also become a part of mainstream culture.

Mindfulness has graced the covers of *Time*, *Scientific American*, and *National Geographic* and has been covered on almost every major news channel. You can even find scenes of Homer Simpson, Ross Geller, Leslie Knope, Squidward Tentacles, Don Draper, and many more beloved fictional characters meditating on TV.

After a half century of academic researchers and mindfulness practitioners working together to clarify the picture, we know a fair bit. There's still a lot unknown, so of course this work must continue, yet the times are also calling younger generations to explore a different collision: the one between mindfulness and technology.

The biggest tech products in the world are designed to narrow your attention. They try to create involuntary mindless habit loops, like constantly swiping down to refresh a feed. Mindfulness pulls in the opposite direction. It's all about opening to a wider awareness. From a more expansive place, you notice when your attention narrows and skillfully choose whether to let it happen or to intervene, all without the friction of self-judgment.

We live in a system that exploits your mental energy for profit. Those that win the attention economy reliably choreograph your mind in ways that help them, not you. The news media profits from polarizing statements. Content creators make millions from views, likes, and subscribers. Businesses drive sales when they keep employees connected at all hours of the day. Politicians fight viciously for airtime to influence voters and gain power.

As this system continues to push your mental capacity to its limit, **attention activism** is a call to reclaim your mind—and your tech—by staying aware of the forces pulling at your attention and making more intentional choices about where you direct it. In the attention economy, this is a radical act.

Mindfulness is not only about spirituality and self-care; it is also an essential tool to exercise your right to freedom of attention. Whether it's breathing or a viral video, a mantra or a meme, attention activists reclaim choice in what to pay attention to. The next generation of mindfulness teachers must teach us not to run away from digital life but to master it as part of who we are.

From each of our subjective points of view, life seems to be nothing more than a sequence of things we pay attention to. A series of momentary experiences. The attention economy is disrupting our waking lives at this most fundamental level. Yet we cannot reclaim attention without reclaiming our tech too. It's only by reclaiming both that we will get out of our own way, preserve freedom, and find well-being in modern life.

TRY: FULLY ENJOYING TECHNOLOGY

When you've got a moment to explore, try fully enjoying a technology that makes you happy. It's so easy to get wrapped up in the idea of what you should and shouldn't be doing. This little practice is an antidote to that. Let yourself enjoy something!

Step 1: Choose a technology that brings you joy. It can be hard to stay present with something that changes a lot, so ideally, choose something with a slower pace. For example, if you love stand-up comedy, find a video of a longer performance instead of a bunch of short clips.

Step 2: Put away all your distractions. Set up your experience by queuing up the tech and putting away anything that might distract you. So if you're watching a TV show, put your phone and tablet away, and maybe even ask anyone you live with for some privacy.

Step 3: Enjoy the experience fully. If you want, you can start with a few deep breaths, maybe even with your eyes closed. When you're ready, start interacting with the tech and see if you can stay present with how it makes you feel.

It helps to take it slow. For example, if you're playing a video game, take your time and notice any feelings, thoughts, or impulses that might arise as you play.

Step 4: Let go of shame, guilt, and doubt. If any thoughts or feelings come up about how you might be wasting your time, how weird this practice feels, or even your ability to stay aware, let that come and go. No need to resist it, but don't dive into it either. Stay with your moment-to-moment experience of the technology.

Step 5: Let positive emotions flow. If any positive thoughts or feelings come up, pay close attention to them and let them flower. So for example, if you're listening to a podcast and someone says something funny, see if you can fully enjoy that without reservation.

Step 6: Stop when you're ready, but no sooner. Some experiences have a natural end, like a TV show. Others you might need to find your own end for, such as browsing a social media feed. In any case, avoid ending the practice at the first moment of resistance. See if you can give it time to run its course. Ride a few ups and downs. When you're done, turn off your tech and take a moment to breathe, reflect, or meditate before moving on.

3

THE NATURE OF TECHNOLOGY

When I first started meditating, I was banging my head against the wall, trying to silence my mind. I was so harsh with myself because I was desperate. I was numb and lost, and I thought that if only I could stop thinking, everything would be bliss. So I gritted my teeth and tried to force my mind to shut up.

My practice opened up when I gave up on trying so hard to clear my mind. I learned to embrace thoughts as a natural and expected part of the human experience, because they are. Sometimes challenging, sometimes useful, sometimes silly—I accept my thoughts. I let them come and go as if they were clouds passing in the sky.

Turns out the idea that thinking is a problem was just another passing thought.

Many of us get caught in a similar pattern with our tech. In the modern world, trying to completely stop using technology feels a lot like trying to stop thinking. Some inspirational quote from a yoga teacher on social tells you to "clear your mind," and not only is that impossible, but it also generates a ton of unnecessary guilt and shame. When more thoughts inevitably come, you beat yourself up for failing. You start to think you're broken.

There are technologies out there that respect your attention, and even some that restore it, but they are certainly not the norm. We're mostly swimming in a cornucopia of mindless, triggering tech that narrows our awareness and erodes our patience.

The more tech disrupts our lives, the more we blame it for everything. We get desperate for freedom and try to disconnect. But tech is so integrated into modern life that it's not long before we need to reconnect. The pendulum swings back and forth as we spiral into shame and self-judgment for being so attached to the very devices we depend on.

Mindfulness is a way out, and acceptance is the first step. In this chapter, we will lay the foundation for a mindful relationship with technology. Instead of resisting tech and disconnecting completely, we will accept all its pitfalls and possibilities as a part of our nature, just like thinking.

DON'T PLAY THE VICTIM

Blaming technology for all our problems is the same mistake we make when we try to force ourselves to stop thinking. In the same way meditators learn to befriend their thoughts, we can work gently and gradually toward finding a middle way with technology. It won't necessarily be easy, but awareness is mysterious, powerful, and always present. Tap into it directly and you just might be able to conquer a few tugs from devious little apps that are trying to manipulate you. If that feels impossible, you may need formal meditation to train up in meta-awareness. If even *that* feels impossible, it might be time to set boundaries or delete a few apps (see chapter 9).

Certainly, corporations need to design more ethically, scientists need to continue researching the impact on mental health and well-being, and lawmakers need to consider if regulation can help. But in the meantime, you are not powerless. Right here, right now, you can stand up for your right to point your mind in whichever direction you damn well please. Pessimists who claim we are all victims of forces larger than ourselves love to convince everyone they're realists, but this is a battle being waged in the mundane moments of everyday life. You have choice. Even if you don't have the power to influence your family, community, organization, or lawmakers, you don't have to give up on your own mind.

Whether you choose to put the devices away today, or whether you choose to spend the whole day in front of a screen, there's nothing to be ashamed of. A little bit of guilt can help you stick to your intentions, but if you're constantly feeling bad about yourself, there are better ways. It's easy to drown in guilt when you wake up from a digital trance and realize you've spent the whole day online. It's just as easy to feel guilty for disconnecting, missing messages, or falling behind on social media and news.

Is there ever a moment to just . . . not feel guilty? Even when glued to a screen, you are worthy just as you are. No shame necessary. No need to beat up on yourself. Accept the part of you that loves tech *and* the part that wants to lock it away. While you're at it, accept your loved ones, even when they ignore you for their screens. No need to harshly punish your kids, or shame other people just for living a modern life. Accept people both younger and older, even if their relationship with tech looks alien to you.

From this foundation of acceptance, pay close attention to how tech shapes you. Forgive yourself when it captures you, because it most definitely will. See clearly how it happened, and you can get better at seamlessly moving between offline and online worlds without getting stuck. It is possible to live a mindful digital life.

You don't have to retreat to the mountains or switch to a dumbphone to find balance. By all means, take an offline day when you need it. Or head off to a retreat center. Hell, go to India and find yourself. I certainly got a lot out of retreating over the years. Time apart from your everyday routine can help you break compulsive habits and find new perspectives. But don't let the benefits of a temporary digital detox distract you from learning how to use tech well in everyday life.

NATURE VERSUS ARTIFICE

When we get overwhelmed, we often say we want to "get out in nature" or go on a "nature walk," but we are just as natural as the birds and the trees. So is the fly buzzing around your garbage can and the mold growing on old fruit. Nature is not somewhere out there. It's everywhere. So where exactly are we trying to go?

We think of our modern lives as artificial, but is that really true? For the past two years, in the spring, a robin has built a nest on top of the light fixture beside my front door. Every time we step out of our home, she squawks to protect her hatchlings. My little boy and I love keeping tabs on Mrs. Robinson.

Inside the house holding up that nest, my family and I cook in a sophisticated kitchen and fiddle with temperature controls. We watch TV, use social media, play video games, and work on laptops. It all feels very different from a nest, but the way we source materials from our natural environment to build these modern lives is not so different from a bird gathering sticks, though certainly on a different scale.

It can be useful to reframe our technological wonders as natural. We imagine our civilization as somehow removed from the wild world. We love to think we're special, but you probably accept that *you* are a part of nature. So why wouldn't your nest be natural too, just like Mrs. Robinson's?

If this feels off, you might be idealizing Mother Nature. Remember, she can be just as destructive as she can be harmonious. There is infinite wonder in the ocean, trees, and skies, but there are also viral infections, natural disasters, and predators killing their prey. When I describe our tech as natural, I'm certainly not saying it's all good.

These days, we yell at our kids to put away their phones while lost in our own. We glance to check a text and end up scrolling for hours. We go down rabbit holes on social until we feel inadequate. We skim polarizing headlines until it feels like the world is on fire. We compulsively reply to work emails on our day off.

Some days we feel more used than user.

But tech is also beautiful, wonderful, and awe-inspiring. It connects us in ways previously thought impossible. It can bring us so much joy. It can help us be productive and organized. We can express ourselves like never before. I use it to stay in touch and collaborate with people across the planet. I use it to listen to and make music. And yes, I even use it to meditate.

You might love smartphones and the social internet. If that's you, it can be hard to admit to the problems without getting defensive. Or you might be someone who hates the way your devices interfere with every moment. You might feel like they're running your life—or worse, *ruining* your life. You might even notice how they're causing harm to people you care about. If you're the type who wants to escape and live on a mountain somewhere, it can be hard to admit how amazing technology can be.

Accepting tech as part of who we are means acknowledging that it's not some foreign, alien invader. It's neither good nor evil. It's us. Even the AIs that seem more independent than ever before depend on the text and images we feed them. They don't exist without us. The internet is a powerful extension of our minds. It amplifies our flaws as much as our strengths. To have a better relationship with technology, we need a better relationship with ourselves.

This is where the issue becomes spiritual.

Tech isn't just nature, it's *human* nature. And these days, it's getting exhausting. With our minds constantly plugged in to amplifiers, it's never been more important to find balance. Our tech mirrors our own values back at us in a distorted way, often causing the opposite effect of what we intend. It isolates us as much as it connects us. It numbs us as much as it inspires us. It bores us as much as it entertains us.

Sometimes we just want to run away from all the emails, feeds, and desperate pleas to like and subscribe.

We want to escape the news. And social media. And online shopping and porn and video games and those group chats where everyone keeps misunderstanding each other. When we say we want to "get out in nature," what we really mean is that we want to get away from human nature. We want to escape who we are.

Understandable. Our brains are plugged in to a billion other brains, each having tens of thousands of thoughts per day. Many organize to profit from all this, designing greedy, distracting, stressful apps—weapons of mass distraction. On the other hand, many also work to make the hive mind useful, fun, and powerful. Unfortunately, both sides produce a ton of unintended consequences.

Experts are studying technology's effects on our mind, trying to regulate its use and establish standards for designing ethical, humane tech. Where does that leave the rest of us? What if you're not a decision-maker? What if you don't have any influence on science, government, media, or tech? Do you just have to sit and wait, hoping they figure it out? Of course not.

Our job is to become aware of how tech affects us and those we care about. We can choose to be better users of technology in everyday life. We can become more discerning about the tech we pay attention to, setting boundaries around apps that exploit us, but also unapologetically delighting in the experiences that bring us joy, improve our lives, and transform us for the better.

It feels like a big job, especially when compulsive screen time can feel completely out of our control. Tech companies can be manipulative. Unethical decision-makers need to face consequences. Still, there's no need to give up and wait for someone to save you. With tech constantly demanding our attention and overwhelming us, your well-being is becoming more and more dependent on the quality of your relationship with it. If mindfulness has taught me anything, it's that you *always* have a choice in how you relate to whatever you experience.

At this point, there's more than enough of a case to at least experiment with some new strategies and see how they impact your life. The experiment doesn't have to be big. Simply reframing how you think about tech can get you pretty far.

CUPCAKES ARE NOT EVIL

I love fresh-baked goods. Cupcakes, cinnamon buns, croissants, cookies—so tasty! I can skip the candies and the gummies pretty easily, but I find it hard to contain myself around all the sweet, doughy stuff. It's a challenge, but is it evil? No, definitely not. We all know this stuff has a ton of sugar and can be bad for you, but it's not innately immoral. Baked goods are delicious and can bring a lot of joy too!

This is a good metaphor for technology. There are a lot of great things about tech. If you can't keep your eyes on the road, though, maybe there's a problem. If you're ignoring the people you care about, maybe there's a problem. If you're watching a movie on your TV while shopping online with your laptop and texting using your phone all at once, there might be a problem.

When I speak about this, I often find that people are immediately able to disclose if a specific habit or app is becoming a problem. I'll start hedging, describing how technology isn't inherently evil. I'll say it's different for everyone, and we each need to decide what's right for us, and then they will interrupt me: "Oh, TikTok for sure. I definitely need to quit TikTok." Many of us already know what's hooking us and what we want to change about our relationship with it. So, why is it so hard to do?

Technology, just like cupcakes, can throw us off balance. There's nothing wrong with having one cupcake, but if you put a tray of them out on the table, I can barely stop myself. My body craves sugar, carbs, and fat specifically because my ancestors found this stuff rare and useful.

It's especially hard to eat healthily when businesses are incentivized to exploit those cravings for profit. We subtract nutritional value for mass production. We even disguise cupcakes as triple-chocolate muffins and pretend milkshakes are coffee so we can sneakily sell them in the morning.

A lot of our mainstream tech exploits our emotional needs in much the same way. Tech can give us an immediate sense of companionship and social connection. It can strengthen our reputation and even make us rich and famous. We can enjoy the thrill of the hunt, find sexual satisfaction, and go looking for love with a few swipes. We can find answers to all our questions. It's all right there.

Often these emotional needs run deeper than tech can go. You think you're connecting with people, you think you're joining a cause, you think you're skilling up on something important, but it's hard to tell if the progress you're making is real. At the end of the day, you might find yourself euphoric or just alone, empty, and unsatisfied with the game you won, the hearts you got on that post, or the client you just landed. If you pay close enough attention, you'll notice that neither of these extremes feels very healthy. Remember, brute force is not the way. Self-criticism isn't helpful. The key is learning to see these patterns in real time. With self-awareness, we can make better choices in the moment.

Is this a day to hold to strict boundaries, or is this a day to open up and let go? Is this a day to disconnect completely? Or is this a day to fully lean into digital life? Even occasional glimpses of what's going on with your mind, body, and technology should be enough to make course corrections, navigating you closer to that sweet spot in every unique day.

Finding a lifestyle where you embrace tech's potential to improve your life without numbing out on digital is not an easy needle to thread. But one thing's for sure: cupcakes are not evil. Yes, we can mass produce them in a manipulative way. And yes, I can overindulge. They can even throw me into tense loops of self-judgment and shame. But it would be just as much of a shame to abandon them completely, because in moderation, cupcakes are delightful and delicious.

Sweets and technology both have incredible power and influence on us precisely because they are so biologically relevant. Still, a mindful relationship doesn't necessarily mean total abstinence. Once in a while, you should be able to have your cupcake and enjoy it too.

IT'S OKAY TO ENJOY THINGS

My love affair with technology started when I was three. My father brought home a big paper bag and set it on the kitchen table. He pulled the bag open to reveal a big black box. It was huge. I had no idea what I was looking at, but when I saw my older brother, Neil, explode in excitement, I knew it was going to be special. The packaging depicted a gray, boxy space station floating in space, complete with two control panels. Marked in bold, rounded letters on the front was a word I'd never seen before: "Nintendo." An hour later—after Neil's turn, of course—I was playing *Super Mario Bros.* on the NES for the very first time. Ever since then, I've been mesmerized.

Video games were the first technology I experienced that could reliably absorb my mind at the push of a button. I loved the immediate feedback loop between my hands on the controller, the audiovisual experience, and the clever challenges I had to overcome. Many years later, as I studied and designed technology myself, I started to understand that most mainstream tech leverages this same kind of rewarding feedback loop.

I'll let the scientists and philosophers debate whether we call it hyperfocus, flow, immersion, or experiential fusion. The point is, with the right balance of effort and reward, tech can absorb our awareness, immersing us completely in a digital world. This can be delightful and magical, but we can also lose track of time, our bodies, our intentions, and the physical world around us. Whether we're joyfully smooshing Goombas, letting the next video autoplay, or even crushing our to-do list, a powerful momentum emerges that can be so hard to stop. The state of mind can be so inherently rewarding and absorbing that it's hard to notice when it becomes an unhealthy fixation. Afterward, we might feel fine, or we might be totally drained and irritable.

These are hard patterns to manage in daily life. These

days, I'm finding it even harder because I'm managing them for two. My little boy is in love with a little pink puffball named Kirby. In fact, I just took a break from writing to ask him if he wanted to play an extra few minutes of video games today or if he wanted a cupcake. Guess which option he chose.

Tech can feel that good. But I can't say this enough: *There's nothing wrong with feeling good.* In fact, enjoying things can even give us more energy to take care of ourselves. It only becomes a problem when we get so attached to that feeling that our lives fall completely out of balance. A device that satisfies a specific lacking emotional need is so powerful that it can lead us to distraction, disconnection, disinformation, dysregulation, and even disease.

To avoid the pitfalls, we acknowledge which technologies influence us for the better and which ones make our lives worse. This is the clarity we need to effectively manage our information diet. As attention activists, we do our best to purposefully choose what we allow to pull at our attention. We take note of the apps that feel more like traps. We limit that which exploits our base urges in moments of weakness.

From there, you can drop the fight. Accept tech as a natural part of who you are. Let go of the shame and guilt as you freely find joy and transformation online. Passionately seek out tech that helps you be who you truly want to become. It is absolutely possible to benefit from tech without letting it exploit you. We do this not because we hate technology but because we love it.

We're cyborgs now. That part isn't really up to you. It's a consequence of being born in the twentieth or twenty-first century. With tech dominating our lives and the lives of people we care about, we have no choice but to use it more skillfully. Our spiritual quest for this information age is to become a *better* cyborg. To reframe your relationship with tech is to reframe your relationship with yourself. This is human nature, amplified.

TRY: CLARIFYING YOUR MOTIVATION

We've covered a lot so far. What part of all this feels motivating to you? Setting a clear intention for why you do something will help you stay with it.

Step 1: Choose whether to meditate or journal. Either find a quiet space where you can sit in silent contemplation or grab a pen and paper to journal your thoughts. Whatever feels natural.

Step 2: Consider your why. Think or write about why you are personally interested in a better relationship with tech. What motivates you? Is there anything specific you're trying to change? How might this shift positively impact not only yourself but also the people around you?

Step 3: Keep asking why. If you have a hard time getting to deeper answers, try asking "why" over and over again like young children do. For example, if you are motivated because you want to be less stressed, you might ask, "Why do I want to be less stressed?" If your answer is because you want to be more present for people you care about, you might ask, "Why do I want to be more present for them?" This can help you find deeper personal truths.

Step 4: Stay in a positive frame. Notice if any judgment or shame comes up, and let it come and go. For example, you might ask "why" and hear your inner voice get self-critical. No need to resist it, but don't give it more energy either. Stay curious and focus on motivations that encourage positive growth.

Step 5: Distill your motivation into a word or phrase. Find something that captures the essence of what motivates you to form a better relationship with tech. Be specific and concise. Memorize your intention or write it down in a visible place as a reminder of your commitment.

4

A DAY IN THE DIGITAL LIFE

If consciousness is a stream, meditation is like climbing up on the riverbank and watching how it flows. In the age of smartphones, AI, and social media, that's not so easy anymore. What are we supposed to do when the stream floods with information?

Even if you do manage to find a few minutes to meditate in the midst of an overstimulated day, you might find it hard to beat the current and climb out. Ten minutes a day hardly seems enough. Even if you do step out of the river, I'm not so sure you'll be able to dry off, catch your breath, and still have the time to get a clear look at the movements of your mind.

Trying to practice mindfulness in the attention economy can feel impossible. You suddenly hit the brakes on a breakneck pace of life, and it feels more like whiplash than any kind of awakening. It's hard enough just to put down the plates we're juggling and find calm, let alone do the deep, subtle work of meditation.

People often say they can't meditate. They try a short,

guided meditation and find their mind to be an overwhelmingly busy place. "I can't stop thinking," they tell me. "I just feel more overwhelmed."

When they ask me how to shut their brain up, I first point out that the goal is not to shut it up at all. Second, I ask, "What's going on the other twenty-three hours and fifty minutes of your day?"

We can try to fight the raging current and swim upstream, we can give up and let it take us, or we can try a third option: building a boat. A mindful relationship with technology is all about learning how to find balance between resisting and completely immersing yourself in digital life. It might take some practice to learn how to be, but with some effort and skill, we can float.

A lot of this tech might be new, but finding balance is not. The historical Buddha famously preached a middle way, but he wasn't the only one. In the foundations of Western thought, Aristotle portrayed virtue as a golden mean: the balance point between two extremes. He saw generosity as a center between greed and wastefulness. Courage was portrayed in between cowardice and recklessness.

We seem to be struggling to find a golden mean with our tech. Attention activism is about moderation. It's about finding the middle ground between self-denial and overindulgence. Whether you like it or not, a lot of modern life takes place online. With so many preaching the extremes, it can be hard to remember that balance is possible.

It is.

We can't let our worst instincts dominate the vibrant realm of diverse relationships we call the internet. As long as we learn how to wield it with awareness, tech can be incredibly fun, creative, and useful. The better we get at using it skillfully, the better we can model wise use for future generations. Giving up is not the way forward.

In the rest of this chapter, I will share five vignettes exploring what balance might look like for a knowledge worker using things like email, calendars, social media, video games, and news. A mindful relationship with tech will look different for everyone, so no need to try to replicate these strategies in your life, especially if you live a different lifestyle. Just let them inspire you to reflect on your own aspirations. And take note of areas where you feel reactive or skeptical; those are a good source of insight too.

A MINDFUL RELATIONSHIP WITH TECHNOLOGY

1: Gradual Awakening

Asleep in bed, you hear a sound. It's the opening to one of your favorite albums. You chose this music specifically because this is the vibe you want to start each day. Your phone is in another room. So instead of getting stressful information first thing in the morning, you wake up to beautiful, familiar music playing automatically on a speaker.

You don't turn it off. You hum along with the melody as you start your morning routine. Maybe you stretch, or put the kettle on, or take a step outside for a deep breath of fresh air. Or maybe you have time for none of that, as you are focused on getting the kids ready for school. Either way, you aren't using your phone at all yet.

During breakfast, you check the news. You don't want to lose yourself in whatever controversies are trending, so you grab a paper magazine. The good thing about paper is that it's inert. You see nothing of today's flash-in-the-pan, gotcha controversy. Nothing you see has been algorithmically tuned to your data profile. Instead, you read an in-depth article analyzing a big news event from last month.

You still haven't looked at a screen yet.

Eventually, a legitimate, practical need comes up. Maybe you need to check your calendar for the day, or see if the bus is on time, or confirm something. You head over to your desk, where your phone has been parked overnight to keep it out of your way. After a fairly complete morning routine, you finally unlock your phone, ready to face the digital world.

2: Self-Awareness at Work

When you start your workday, the first thing on your calendar is a block of time you've booked with yourself specifically to clear your inbox. You've done this for a few important reasons.

First of all, you don't have work email on your phone, so you didn't check it last night or this morning. You prioritize reviewing email early in case anyone's waiting on you. On top of that, you like taking time to respond thoughtfully to people. It's easy to rapid-fire replies, but you've learned that taking the time to send clear, concise, and direct emails avoids so many downstream conflicts and miscommunications.

Another reason to start with email is to reduce its power to distract you later in the day. Getting it out of the way first helps you stay focused on other things. After you clear your inbox, you find yourself better able to engage and pay full attention to whatever's next.

During your lunch break, you spend some time outside. It's a beautiful day. You know you have a call with your colleague after lunch. This is someone you trust, so you send her a quick text: "Walking meeting?" She enthusiastically agrees, so you toss your headphones in and head out on a walk. You end up both spending the better part of an hour discussing your personal lives and work details, even turning your camera on at one point to share a beautiful vista. You're getting better acquainted, getting things done, getting those steps in, and getting some sun.

At the end of the day, you check your email one last time, but you don't send any replies. This is another nuance you've discovered about yourself. If you send emails at the end of the day, you've noticed that your mind races in the evening. You tend to ruminate on whatever you sent and compulsively check for replies.

And if you actually get a reply that night, instead of satisfying you, it usually ends up triggering more thoughts and often leads you to work into the evening and late at night. So at the end of the day, maybe you write a few drafts, but you don't send anything until the morning.

3: Enjoying Authentic Connection
At some point during the day, you hear a ding. You immediately know it's a text, and you know who it's from. That's because you've disabled sound notifications for everyone except two important people in your life. You pull out your phone and respond to the message. Seems everything is okay.

You've got a few minutes, so while you've got your phone out, you opt in to checking what else is waiting for you. You have no idea what's there because nothing on your phone has permission to show up on your lock screen, vibrate, or make a sound. In other words, nothing's ever allowed to interrupt you. The only exceptions are phone calls from anyone and texts from those two important people.

When you unlock your phone, everything looks the same as it always does except for a single aggregate number showing how many notifications you have across the few select apps you allow to notify you. Today, it's seven—seven unread messages from a few different apps. It's just one combined number because you've grouped those apps together. No matter what's happening in your digital life, you only ever see this single number change, and you only see it after you unlock. No message previews, banners, or anything like that.

You take a moment to read and reply. You end up sharing some video messages with loved ones, some of which you haven't seen in a long time. Video and sound make the connection feel closer than text. You're also happy to see that a few people engaged with your last post. That always feels good, and you enjoy it.

Some of these reactions come from friends you've never met IRL but have connected with online over the years. These are people with whom you have never had a physical interaction. They can't give you a hug. You don't know what they look like. You're not even sure if they know who you are. Yet their reactions mean a lot because you share an understanding about niche interests that you can't find with anyone in your everyday life.

4: Deleting a Sticky App in the Moment

After work, you go for a walk and see a beautiful sunset. You yank out your phone and take a picture to share it on your favorite social network. As you continue on your walk, you think back for a second. *I didn't really enjoy that view.*

The reality is you barely looked at it because you immediately pulled out your phone. You don't judge yourself for this. It's fun to share a beautiful moment with your people. But you did notice a pattern. This wasn't the first time. This particular social app keeps leading you to commodify your experience.

Instead of enjoying the sunset, you treated it like a means to an end. It was a great social post and started some fun conversations, but still, you kinda missed the actual sunset. You decide to delete the app, and you do so immediately, before you have a chance to overthink it.

It's not that the app is evil or anything. Many enjoy it, and you'll still enjoy it on your laptop. But with a little self-awareness over time, you clearly see why having it on your phone is not a great fit for you. You set a boundary, not because you're anti-tech but because you love sunsets.

Over time, you continue to remove apps when you notice them becoming too sticky. With careful curation, your phone has become a positive force in your life. You're able to use and enjoy it more fully specifically because you put a limit on the patterns that tend to hook you.

5: Winding Down with a Video Game

As your responsibilities fade and you wind down for the day, you park your phone back on your desk. It's charging in a designated place to make sure it's out of your way at night and in the morning.

You're tired and probably going to head to sleep soon, but there's nothing wrong with a little play to help you unwind. You decide to fire up your gaming console, and a few titles pop up that you've been enjoying lately.

There's a triple-A, story-driven single-player action game; an aesthetically beautiful indie; and a clever puzzle game. You also see a competitive action game and the twitchy shoot-em-up that you love playing with your friends online.

This seems like a trivial choice, but you know it's not. You've been training yourself to be mindful of how games, movies, and TV shows affect you. Over time, you've realized that how you entertain yourself in the evening affects your state of mind at night and the next morning.

You immediately rule out the frantic, fast-paced options because you know they have the power to hook you and demolish your sleep. They're better for the weekend. The puzzle game can be relaxing, but you've been doing a lot of conceptual work today and you know your mind needs a break from solving problems.

The calming indie game seems the mindful choice, but somehow you're not feeling it today. There's a lot going on at work, and you know it's going to be too slow to short-circuit your work thoughts. You'll probably just half-play it while ruminating about your projects.

So that leaves the story-driven action game. It should be just enough to engage you, but it's unlikely to hook you or overactivate your nervous system just before bed. You load up the game. It's fun and relaxing, and you enjoy it. You lose yourself in it.

Once in a while, you check in with your body, adjusting your posture a bit, noticing how the game is affecting you, and maybe taking a deep breath. After a while, a gentle alarm sounds from the TV, reminding you not to play too late. You dismiss the alarm and decide to finish this level. When you get to the next checkpoint, you honor your intention, turn off the TV, and head to bed.

You don't stop to check your phone on the way.

SEVEN LENSES TO EXPERIMENT WITH

These are glimpses into an everyday modern life where tech is integrated with awareness and a spirit of experimentation. These are not stories of disconnection and strict abstinence, yet they aren't tales of compulsive use either. These are stories of balance.

Your life might be very different from these vignettes. Your pendulum might be swinging in a different direction these days. It's all good. People are diverse, and things change over time. The specific details aren't the point. What matters is that a mindful relationship with technology is all about paying close attention to how different tech affects you and using that insight to fearlessly experiment in your own life.

That being said, peppered throughout these stories are a few specific strategies that apply more generally to different life circumstances. We'll focus on these in the second half of the book.

Staying present while working on a laptop, watching TV, or using your phone can be a tall order. Thankfully, the goal isn't to stay perfectly grounded in every moment. Even just glimmers of noticing can be fascinating and useful. If you're overwhelmed, take it slow and let change naturally arise.

As I've mentioned, there are certain circumstances where you need to be extra careful. As Jonathan Haidt has pointed out, if you're under sixteen, tech may disrupt critical periods for social and cultural development. As Dan Siegel discusses in *Brainstorm*, if you're under twenty-five, your brain isn't considered fully developed, including its capacity for self-regulation. If you're dealing with clinical-grade depression, anxiety, addiction, insomnia, or self-harm, some forms of tech can be especially harmful. If you are neurodivergent in ways that are relevant to attention and social life, the relationship with tech you need might look very different.

In any of these situations, the strategies in the next few chapters will still be very useful, but they might also land differently or be harder to implement. Your mileage may vary, and you may need additional support. As I've mentioned, these strategies are not a substitute for professional mental health care, and they aren't tailored to deliver the many things children need for proper development.

That being said, what follows will help you mitigate and minimize the negative impact of technology and strengthen the positive. These are strategies to make sure you don't feel inadequate, your attention isn't dominated, and you aren't getting stuck on illusions. They're also going to help you find authentic digital connection, enjoy digital entertainment, and leverage tech for well-being.

The reality is that technology can have an incredibly powerful impact on our quality of life for better *and* worse. The research is showing a lot of negative impacts in the very same categories where mindfulness shows positive impacts. In many ways, establishing a mindful digital lifestyle is a direct response to what's happening to us as technology eats the world.

It might seem like hard work, but if you've read this

far, you've done the hard part. Understanding how mindfulness can serve as an antidote to the attention economy will naturally lead to different choices. The minimum you need to do is simply remember what you're learning here, get out of your own way, and let change happen.

My hope is that the foundation we've been building has you fired up and feeling ready to go beyond that minimum and dive in fully to the next seven chapters. They each spell out a unique strategy for interacting with technology skillfully and mindfully. While reading through these strategies will lead to gradual change, you have the option to take them off the page and apply them fully to the mundane moments of your everyday life. I'm confident you can find a rhythm that works for you without fear, shame, or unnecessary guilt.

TRY: COMMITTING TO ONE CHANGE

Some of the ideas in this chapter may have felt applicable to your life, some not so much. Now it's time to expand beyond the hypothetical. Take this opportunity to consolidate that learning and commit to experiment with making a change in your actual life.

Step 1: Reflect on examples that resonated. Write down or contemplate any ideas, moments, or vignettes from this chapter that felt inspiring to you. Notice if any of the examples are still banging around in your head. Are those directions you aspire to in your own relationship with technology?

Step 2: Identify examples that didn't align. Next, identify any examples that felt off to you. If anything didn't align with your lifestyle, that's okay. To understand the kind of relationship you want to have with tech, you also need to clarify the kind of relationship you *don't* want to have.

Step 3: Visualize a better relationship. Imagine or write about what an aspirational relationship with tech could look like for you personally. Explore key moments in your daily routine, like waking up, working, being in transit, leisure time, and going to bed.

Step 4: Commit to making one change. It's better to make a small change and succeed than make a big commitment and fail. So don't try to do everything at once, especially if you're new to this kind of thing. Pick one specific tweak to experiment with, something light and easy, like changing your morning alarm, going for a walking meeting, or unsubscribing from something.

Step 5: Take action now. Go set up your new commitment immediately. Now is the moment when you're motivated and inspired, so this is the best time to get that app off your phone, update your calendar, or move your phone charger. If there isn't any setup required, write a note to yourself and post it somewhere visible.

PART TWO

SEVEN STRATEGIES

5

START WITH AWARENESS

> When we open to the reality of what is, even if we don't like what is, it helps almost immediately.
>
> —Kristin Neff

When I first learned what the attention economy was doing to our minds, I was angry. I got especially angry when I saw it in my own life and affecting those around me. When I saw family, friends, and even strangers using tech, I took a holier-than-thou attitude, like I was Morpheus and they were stuck in the Matrix. I took an aggressive attitude with myself too, setting strict rules and harshly judging myself when I broke them.

It's funny how we judge others for the exact things we struggle with ourselves. I did this with no one more than my own wife. At the time, I'm sure I believed I was a knight in shining armor, saving Krista from nefarious tech supervillains. In reality, I think I just wanted her to pay attention to me and hated that her phone was getting in the way. So instead of telling her that I cared about her or that I felt lonely, I'd end up mansplaining the attention economy. Not ideal.

I didn't realize I was doing this until we became parents and had a lot less time and energy for each other. Eventually my wife was brave enough to tell me how guilty I made her feel when she was using her phone. It was an eye-opening moment. I realized that, although I was justifiably angry about the attention economy and what it was doing to all of us, my resistance against it was turning me into an insufferable prick.

After that insight, whenever I'd come downstairs after putting our son to bed and see her with her phone, I'd notice my reaction, let it pass, and give her more space and time for herself. I also found myself naturally cutting friends, family, and even strangers more slack. I became less self-critical about my own tech use too. I stopped pushing so hard, and a gentler, more natural change began to take place.

What's fascinating is that this transformation didn't really take much effort. I became aware of a pattern, and that awareness led to better choices. When my outrage toward these devices showed up in an unhealthy way, I'd notice it in the moment just a little bit, and that was enough to make a difference.

Just by noticing the pattern, it began to weaken. Awareness can lead to effortless change. That's why it's the first strategy we'll focus on in our quest for a better relationship with technology.

SOMETIMES AWARENESS IS ENOUGH

When you become aware of something, it becomes a part of your subjective world. You start to notice it more, and this naturally starts to influence your thoughts, actions, and speech. Your experience of it changes, but you also start to interact with it differently. Over time, things can change in a way that feels mysterious and effortless.

If you have challenging emotions around how all this tech is manipulating you or the people around you, it can be so easy to jump right into strategizing and making changes. You might decide that you are going to stop using your phone so much, or that you are going to stop responding to emails on weekends, or that you're going to give up TV. I recommend you hold off on implementing too many big changes all at once.

It can also be easy to start criticizing, complaining, and pointing fingers. I've definitely done my fair share of blaming big corporations, beating myself up for overconsumption, and making those around me feel guilty. The anger and frustration may be justified, but it's not a constructive way forward in our personal lives.

A fulfilling relationship with your devices doesn't have to be difficult, especially if you work with care. Instead of attempting to forcefully change your habits, try widening the scope of your attention and letting awareness create change. Sometimes awareness is enough.

Instead of making changes, for now, seek as much clarity as possible. Open your eyes to what technology really is, what role it plays in your life, and how different apps and devices affect you. Pay attention to what brings you joy and what feels draining.

As you become more aware of how and why you use tech, you may notice things change on their own. This mysterious force is hard to explain, but when it happens, it takes a lot of the burden off your willpower. The more you can stay connected with a more expansive awareness, the less urgent all tech's little tricks and dings and bleeps and bloops will feel.

For now, stay aware. Drop any plan more complicated than this.

AUTOPLAY THE NEXT VIDEO?

If you think this awareness-first approach is magical thinking, let me remind you that attention activism is not about self-optimization but self-care. This is an issue of mental and emotional well-being. It defeats the whole purpose if it comes from strict perfectionism or aggressive restriction.

Trust that awareness will naturally plant seeds for change. Only after those seeds are planted can they flower. There's no point in drowning yourself in negative emotions, taking on the victim mentality, resenting joy, or antagonizing people. It's self-defeating to grind it out. You can't strangle a flower out of a seed. You need to plant it and nurture it. It takes time.

TV is a great place to practice. After watching something online, often you'll see a little timer or progress bar counting down to the next video or episode. When I'm tired and stressed, it's very difficult to resist. There's barely enough time to notice what's happening, let alone muster the willpower to stop my descent deeper into TV land.

There's nothing wrong with watching TV, but if you look closely at this example, you'll notice something missing: choice. I didn't choose to watch the next episode, did I? I did nothing, and the next episode started. Sure, technically I could have stopped it. But if you ask yourself why that countdown timer is there, you'll see the attention economy at work.

When we practice mindfulness, we're training our minds to do the exact opposite of what that timer does. A video, movie, or TV show has a certain forward momentum. Each scene leads to the next. When it ends, the timer preserves that forward momentum. It keeps you narrowly focused on the screen, waiting for the next thing to happen. It's designed to seamlessly bridge you from one video to the next by removing the feeling that something is ending. It deviously tries to prevent you from opening up to a wider awareness and making a new choice.

Until we figure out how to regulate or incentivize big media companies to change these kinds of manipulative design patterns, it's on us to notice. Next time you watch a video, see if you can stay aware as it ends. Let the countdown timer be a cue to broaden your attention and tap into awareness. Zoom out to notice the room around you. Are you tired? How does your body feel? Do you need some water or a quick stretch? What time is it?

As you slow down, you make space for more intention. Even a split second of a more expansive awareness might inspire a choice that truly serves you. Keep in mind that this doesn't necessarily mean you stop watching. Bringing mindfulness to the transition, you might confidently choose to watch the next video and enjoy it. That's an intentional choice too.

When you reflect on how sticky TV can be, at some point you'll probably wonder if you should quit TV altogether. I've tried that, and I must say, it may be helpful for a short period, but I'm not sure it's necessary long term. It might just be another swing of the pendulum. Instead of rushing to big actions, ask yourself where that idea is coming from. If it's emerging from a whole heap of unnecessary guilt, investigate that first.

Are you somehow a bad person if you binge-watch a TV show? Even the term "binge" is full of shame. Why are we beating ourselves up about this? There are some great shows and movies out there! Binge-watching can certainly become mindless, but you can't quit everything, and these patterns are everywhere.

Maybe the better approach is to ask *how* you watch TV. See if you can be slightly more mindful of how your body and mind feel during and after watching. You might feel fine, having experienced a lot of joy and immersion without much cost. You might feel guilty, like you're wasting your time or numbing out. Or you might feel awful, with cramps and brain fog.

Paying close attention to the subtleties of experience will clarify if any changes are necessary. You may see why you need to unsubscribe from a certain service or channel, or you may see there's no need to limit TV at all. Through self-awareness, you can decide for yourself.

It's the mindlessness, not the tech, that prevents us from finding balance. The specific design patterns that encourage mindlessness aren't helping. But from the perspective of awareness, that countdown timer is just a progress bar on a screen. When you see it for what it is in the moment, it loses its power over you.

It's not that streaming services don't give you a lot of choice. They do. It's just that one choice always seems to be buried: turning it off. That's on you.

SELF-TRACKING FOR SELF-AWARENESS

It's easy to imagine awareness as passive, like some kind of receiver. But awareness exerts a subtle yet powerful influence on your thoughts, feelings, and behavior. It reminds me of quantum physics in the way observation mysteriously changes things.

On the quantum level, things get weird. Calculating the state of a quantum system produces an average of all its possible states. Yet actually measuring it collapses the system down to one specific state. From that point on, the system behaves differently. It's hard to even understand.

Imagine if your weather app always gave you an average forecast: partly cloudy with some precipitation at Earth's average temperature of 15°C / 59°F. But whenever you went outside to see how it felt, the weather changed to a different state and stayed that way. You change the forecast just by stepping outside to see how it feels. Like I said: weird.

I've found that awareness works in a similar way. Observation itself has influence.

Just by tapping into a wider awareness, you see things differently. As soon as you notice them, things change. Seeds of insight naturally influence how you relate to yourself, the world around you, and yes, technology. Whatever that insight is about, you'll never see it the same again.

Once, on a meditation retreat, I noticed that my body became extremely tense when thinking about money. It felt relevant to my childhood, as my parents immigrated with very little. The very instant I noticed that pattern, my relationship to money changed forever. My wife would suggest a major purchase, and instead of getting cranky about it, I would notice the tension. Instead of dumping it on Krista, I'd let the challenging emotions pass and respond in a calm way.

While meditation can help you tap into awareness, it's not the only way. Soon after I understood my anxious attachment to money, I started budgeting and tracking our family expenses. It helped us manage our finances in a practical way, but for me, it was also profoundly healing. We don't always have the time or energy for formal meditation practice. Another way to increase awareness is to track yourself.

In 2014, I downloaded two experimental new apps called Checky and Moment that passively tracked my phone use. These apps weren't native to the phone's operating systems. In fact, I literally had to take a screenshot of my settings screen and upload it to Moment to get around the phone's limitations and access my screen-time statistics.

Yet even with these clunky tools, the effect was dramatic. After my first week using them, I was shocked to learn that within a single day, I unlocked my phone over one hundred times and looked at it for more than two hours. I kept tracking, and a few months later, I checked again. Something amazing happened.

Each week, the numbers were getting progressively lower. It went gradually from one hundred checks to thirty checks, and from two hours a day to one hour a day. But the funny thing is, I didn't make any explicit plans or take any action. Yet in all those little moments throughout my day, a little more awareness crept in and gradually changed my habits.

I started to notice when I was tethered to my device, constantly checking work email, news, social media, and more. I saw my habit loops and patterns more clearly. I noticed which apps were sticky, affecting my mood, reducing my sleep, or taking me away from things I care about.

All I was doing was noticing. The only extra effort I put into this was checking the statistics regularly. It was the increased awareness that led to change. Self-tracking made my usage patterns a more salient aspect of my world. I naturally paid more attention to them. Whenever I reached to pick up my phone or stared at it too long, there was a little extra space for me to become aware of my behavior, which naturally led me to respond differently.

I doubt the pioneering attention-activist founders of Checky or Moment got a penny, but these features are now native to most smartphones. They're useless if you don't check them, though. What might happen if you tracked your phone use and checked every day? Or if you kept a diary of your usage schedule, which apps you spend the most time thinking about, and how they make you feel?

By documenting certain aspects of your body, behavior, and experience, you become aware of your own habits. This wider perspective will bring change naturally into your life. Especially if you have limited energy for big changes, in the early stages of improving your relationship with tech, invest in awareness. It's the best bang for your buck.

TRY: MEDITATING ON BODY, WORLD, MIND

Let's tap into awareness right here, right now. These instructions are meant to be followed in real time as you read, so get comfortable.

Step 1: Slow down your reading pace. Often we read frantically, like we're trying to get somewhere. For this section—just as we did at the end of the Introduction—drop that, slow down, and luxuriate on each word. Let go of any temptation to rush through these instructions.

Step 2: Release any tension in your body. As you read, lend a little attention to wherever you feel connection with the ground. Root yourself in body sensations and feelings. If it feels available, open up to your entire body at once, releasing tension wherever you find it.

Step 3: Become aware of the outside world. You can also probably hear other sounds around you. Maybe birds, traffic, or the hum of an appliance. You might also be aware of your peripheral visual field while you slowly read. Notice light, shadow, and color.

Step 4: Notice what's happening in your mind. Listen to your inner voice read these words. Notice the pace, cadence, and even the tone of your inner voice. Notice any other thoughts or mental images that arise, whether in response to the text or not.

Step 5: Pause reading, and soak in awareness. If it feels right, stop reading for a moment and fully soak in an open awareness of whatever's happening in body, world, and mind. Put the book down and take as long as you need. At least a minute. Maybe ten?

Step 6: Transition out of the practice. When you're ready, drop the effort for now. Take a deep breath, stretch, or enjoy a sip of water. See if you can effortlessly carry this awareness forward into the next hour, especially if you'll be interacting with tech.

Step 7: Should you go back to step 1? Did you read this without actually doing it? If so, no judgment. As we've covered, it's getting harder to slow down. Awareness is experiential. It's worth exploring in direct experience, not just thinking about it conceptually. Try again?

6

SEE THROUGH CONCEPTUAL ILLUSIONS

> The more we witness our emotional chain reactions and understand how they work, the easier it is to refrain.
>
> —Pema Chödrön

As I write this book, my mind believes I am "writing" in a "document" saved to "memory." What I'm actually doing is pressing plastic keys that send electrical signals to a computer that lights up pixels to form letters in real time. This text will be stored as magnetic patterns that I will eventually send to print.

Designers have been using interface metaphors like these to simplify how we interact with computers since the beginning. From the "desktop" to the "mouse." From "surfing" the information "highway" to electronic "mail." From the "shopping cart" to "checkout."

We mix clever metaphors with graphic design to create conceptual illusions that define how we interact with our tech. This practical magic is turning out to be a double-edged sword, though. While metaphors usually make most tech easier without cause for concern, using similar conceptual illusions for intimate, personal applications gets a little problematic.

As you practice becoming more aware of how you interact with different technologies, you might notice a few metaphors that seem suspect. Are these people actually "following" you? Does a "match" actually mean two people are a good fit? Do a majority of people actually care about that "trending" news story? Does someone "liking" a post mean they actually read it? Does a "view" mean they watched the whole video? Whether with a human being or an AI, are the messages you're sending back and forth really a "conversation"?

I think you see what I'm getting at here: the reality that our tech serves up is illusory. In some cases, those illusions prey on your emotions to keep you plugged in. Let's take a look at how we can realign our vision to stay grounded in reality and get what we need in a deeper, lasting way.

REALITY ISN'T ALWAYS COMFORTABLE

The most popular technologies tend to reduce uncomfortable realities into comfortable illusions. We feel good when we find easy ways to connect with people and get answers that confirm our beliefs. These conceptual illusions help us stave off discomfort, uncertainty, and loneliness—but they're not always real.

Once you start to see this, you'll see why it might be a problem. Tech initially got mainstream traction because it simplified our lives. Now, it's the biggest industry in the world with a dangerous penchant for *over*simplifying our lives. Reality isn't always comfortable. It can get complex and messy, and it's full of uncertainty. So of course we're eager for media that makes us comfortable, provides easy answers, and demands less social effort.

Messaging apps cut the unpredictability from our relationships. Search engines and news feeds tend to give us the answers we want to hear in personalized echo chambers. Media platforms ignore nuance as they cast clear heroes and villains. Social media give us instant gratification without long-term fulfillment. Video games place us in virtual playgrounds where we don't have to collaborate on defining play with other people, deal with genuine risk, or exert our bodies. And do I even have to write about porn? Let's just say that video illusions can be a fun distraction until they disrupt the real thing. I'll leave it at that.

These can all be useful, entertaining, and engaging technologies, but they're so easy to overdo because they provide illusions that are easier than the truth. Curated relationships, editable identities, sexual pleasure on demand, and a society where everyone agrees with you. Who wouldn't want to sleep forever in such a utopian dream? Except the dream doesn't last.

If we buy into these illusions too much, we struggle when facing reality. It can be hard to connect with a physical life in which we don't get nearly as much control or stimulation as we do online. And if we end up buying into all these emerging virtual and augmented reality headsets, this is only going to get harder.

As we sink deeper into digital life, all of a sudden it's excruciatingly boring to wait for the bus. The idea of your phone running out of battery feels like a waking nightmare. Changing diapers becomes an obstacle to getting back to your phone. And talking to people IRL feels too risky, especially since you can't check their profile or unsend messages you regret.

This is an area where technology is doing us a disservice. A lot of the technologies that have taken root in our society distort our desires. They take things we authentically want, like reputation, information, and conversation, and simulate them in an illusory way. The digital versions seem to placate our conceptual minds, yet somehow at the end of the day, we don't actually feel satisfied.

As a species, our superpower is clear: we cooperate at scale to transform the world, and in turn, transform ourselves. We've used this superpower to create near-telepathic communication networks. Satellites guide our walk to the coffee shop. Algorithms personalize our experience of the world. Artists create world-class videos, music, and video games from their laptops. This is the science fiction of generations past.

Yet as all this tech goes viral, it's reaching into more intimate and important areas of life, and we find ourselves vulnerable. The problem arises when we think we're getting what we need, but we're not. As we'll discuss more in chapter 8, it's fine to have a lot of followers as long as they don't get in the way of making a few actual friends. These illusions can leave us less motivated to pursue deep, lasting solutions.

Why not live in a virtual reality where everything is comfortable, answers come easy, and everything is tailored to serve us? To put it simply, our well-being, personal relationships, and participation in society depend on our ability to be okay off-screen too.

Any technology that threatens your capacity to be okay without that technology has crossed an important line. If tech is making it harder for you to face boredom, discomfort, and uncertainty, there's a problem. Here are the hard truths: life isn't always pleasurable, sometimes there are no answers, and everything definitely isn't about you.

In fact, it's often the discomfort, uncertainty, and friction that makes things meaningful and satisfying. When I dropped out of school to tour in a band, I certainly didn't plan for us to barely make any money before imploding in internal disagreements and a failure to gain traction. Yet I remember that as one of the best years of my life. Working through conflict builds closer relationships. Overcoming adversity and taking risks helps you build confidence and self-esteem. Facing contradictory ideas makes you more realistic in your understanding of the world.

Tech can entertain us and simplify our lives without harm only if we keep track of its illusions. It's okay to spend time in the cloud as long as we don't forget the ground.

IDENTIFYING DEEPER EMOTIONAL NEEDS

When my son, Oliver, was three, he started playing iPad games. He loved these little puzzle apps. There was one where he had to put a square peg in a square hole, a round peg in a round hole, and so on. After a few weeks, I noticed the tablet games were making him cranky in a way that didn't seem to happen when he watched videos. What was different?

I began to watch him carefully. One evening when the iPad was nowhere in sight, I saw him playing with a little plastic toy that was the physical equivalent of his favorite tablet game. It was a plastic box with holes of different shapes, each matched to a corresponding block.

I watched as he picked up the triangle-shaped block and put it on top of the triangle hole. It wasn't angled just right and wouldn't go in. He got very frustrated and threw the block. I suddenly realized why he was getting so cranky.

At first glance, that iPad game seemed harmless enough, maybe even educational. Yet by digitally simplifying his toys, it was teaching him that motor coordination could be easier than it actually is. When he simply dragged the shape vaguely to the right location, it automatically lined up and went in the hole.

Clearly not everyone needs to steer clear of touch screens. For you and I, not having to meticulously position things the way we do in the physical world is convenient. Drag 'n drop is simply a more usable interface. But for a child who is actively struggling to figure out fine motor coordination, it's a very tempting way to avoid an uncomfortable feeling.

Out of all the games on that iPad, Oliver kept coming back to something that was simplifying his biggest challenge in the physical world.

Learning to use hands is not an easy task for children. It's frustrating, and they have to try over and over again before they get it right. The digital simulation let him skip the challenge. Why struggle with fitting an actual square peg in an actual square hole when you can just drag and drop? He must have found it so satisfying to see the peg magically slide in.

As you might have already noticed, this isn't just about

children. We all do this. You can look at any technology you use in your own life and ask the same questions: What uncomfortable feeling is this helping me avoid? What emotional need is it putting a Band-Aid on? This is especially important for the technologies you find hard to resist.

While the evidence shows potential harm for young people, our grown-up digital fixations can seem harmless. Yet with awareness, we may find ourselves stuck on specific conceptual illusions that are helping us escape discomfort and placate emotional needs. You might be surprised to find your stickiest technologies are preventing you from finding deeper, lasting ways to fill the holes in your heart.

What technologies are you stuck on and why? Do you mindlessly scroll short videos because you're overwhelmed by your own thoughts? Do you marathon games because you feel a lack of control over your life? Are you always checking work email because your self-worth depends on productivity? And most importantly, are there better ways for you to address these deep emotional needs?

With awareness, you can identify what's causing you to crave certain technologies. You may find the habit relatively harmless and let it be. Or you may clearly see that you've been feeding emotional pain with digital illusions. You may realize that if you keep scratching that mosquito bite, it'll start to bleed. In that case, address the root cause instead of banging your head against the wall with symptoms.

I've been living this pattern recently, ever since I moved to a new town. I don't know a lot of people here. Tech has been a lifeline to keep me connected with distant family and friends. Yet it also became a crutch that was just satisfying enough to stave off the motivation to make local friends. In the end, it didn't work. Eventually the loneliness caught up to me. It was hard to sleep, and I found myself negative, irritable, and spending more and more of my life online.

Social media platforms are fine additions to an already healthy social life, but those of us struggling to find enough face-to-face connection need to be careful. It's hard to put myself out there and try to make friends in this new town, but I'm making progress. I know that if I try to avoid these uncomfortable feelings and fill this need with digital connection alone, my mood and mental health will start to suffer. Those texts and emojis became empty calories.

Your situation might be different. Social media might be a healthy, fun part of your life. But maybe you find yourself binge-watching travel videos on YouTube instead. You might explore why. Which specific videos are engaging you? When do you tend to watch them? How do you feel when you watch them? You might discover a thirst for adventure, a feeling of boredom, or a fear of missing out.

Once you see an uncomfortable feeling you're trying to avoid with tech, try to identify the underlying emotional need. From there, you might ask whether you can address it in a deeper and more holistic way. Maybe it's time for a road trip or a vacation if you can afford it. Or maybe this isn't about travel, and what you really need is to shake things up locally, maybe learn a new recipe or try a new sport.

Another person's compulsive tech may be totally innocuous for you because you have different emotional needs. The touch screen was an epic innovation that has improved the usability of our devices for the vast majority of people. It just so happened to be problematic for three-year-old Oliver when it got in the way of learning to use his hands.

Tablet games are fun, travel videos are wonderful, and social media can provide so much connection and joy. But if we're using tech to avoid hard things, we might end up trapped, using more and more without ever finding a lasting satisfaction. Clearly seeing the illusion empowers us to address root causes instead of scratching itches.

MOST ADVICE IS NOT FOR YOU

I see a lot of books, videos, and social posts glorifying an analog lifestyle. There are a lot of messages about unplugging accompanied by pictures of beautiful people dressed in white, drinking tea in front of oceans, mountains, and forests. They pretend to advocate for balance and well-being while low-key shaming us for how many hours per day we spend looking at screens.

Ironically, this stuff goes viral on social media. I understand why. The part of me that loves silent meditation retreats is drawn to it. In our modern, connected world, the ideology of disconnection can be so attractive.

Here's yet another illusion to watch out for. It's not much different from influencers who show off their perfect abs, passive income, and hyperproductive morning routines. Much like waking up early to work out, disconnecting in a cabin feels attractive and inspiring. I can't look away. Yet it also makes me feel like there's something wrong with my life. Like I'm not enough.

Online, we see advice and success stories for every area of life, but if you don't understand yourself, the best you can do is try whatever the algorithm serves up at random. Odds are high you'll end up feeling inadequate, comparing your everyday life to curated peak moments from people who don't share your values.

With self-awareness, you can make the right tradeoffs. Someone makes a suggestion, and you can tell immediately if it applies to you. Most of it doesn't. I'm not going to abandon tech and move to the jungle, just like I'm not going to work on my six-pack at six in the morning. These are fine aspirational visions for some minority of people, but they don't line up with my goals in life.

Knowing myself with confidence means I don't need to feel guilty about others' achievements. (Read that again if you need to. I'll wait.)

Seeing through these illusions doesn't make all the advice useless. It just helps you more clearly decide what's relevant for you personally. There are a lot of tips and tricks out there. Self-observation will make it easier to experiment with strategies that fit your lifestyle goals and avoid the ones that don't.

When I followed advice to give up tech altogether, getting rid of my TV, deleting most of my apps, and setting rigid screen limits, it was not sustainable. Disconnecting felt boring and unnecessarily strict for someone who grew up fascinated by technology and found success in knowledge work. I'd always come back to a screen and often felt guilty for failing. Lose-lose.

If you're just putting up with tech and you see it as a hassle, then messages demonizing it might resonate with you. But what if you do a lot of healthy, productive, joyful things on-screen? What if you use it to make music and art, connect with niche communities, or build online businesses? If you love tech, ignore the anti-tech advice and find balance without losing the joy.

When I see someone recommend switching to a dumbphone, I know their advice is not for me. When I see someone demonize social media and video games, or suggest strict screen-time limits with no regard for what I'm doing on that screen, I ignore it. When someone overstates the case, treating apps like opioids when we know actual tech addictions are rare, I get skeptical. I realize that my goals are different from theirs, and that's okay.

On the other hand, when someone offers tips on how to use social media in healthy ways, I listen. When a wellness influencer reviews different apps and games, exploring how they emphasize different values, I watch. When someone helps me more skillfully choose how I want to participate in the digital world and when to take a break, I subscribe.

I seek to heal my relationship with tech, not abandon it.

You can easily find libraries full of information on how to eat well, stay fit, have a successful marriage, develop your career, and, yes, manage your tech. But if you're not careful, you can get trapped chasing someone else's goals. Especially if your age, mental state, or unique profile put you in a special circumstance.

So what about me? Should you listen to the strategies I'm providing? Well, certainly not every specific idea. But if you start with awareness and see through illusions, it will become clear what's worth trying. Yet there's no room for subtlety if you're caught up in a fearmongering moral panic or accelerating techno-optimism. These extremes are conceptual illusions like any other.

Nothing can provide more wisdom for your own personal relationship with technology than closely observing the subtle interactions you have with it in everyday life. Self-awareness is essential to avoid chasing ghosts.

TRY: DIRECTLY ADDRESSING AN EMOTIONAL NEED

When we compulsively use tech to satisfy an emotional need, it often works in a superficial way. Brainstorming deeper ways to more fully meet your emotional needs can help reduce your attraction to conceptual illusions.

Step 1: Think of a type of technology you use compulsively. Start by reflecting on or writing down an example of something you find yourself using more than you'd like. No need to feel guilty about it. Just notice what comes up with curiosity.

Step 2: Identify feelings you're avoiding and underlying emotional needs. Why do you use this technology? What uncomfortable feelings might you be trying to avoid? What deeper emotional need might be at the root of this pattern? If you can't stop refreshing your work email, you might be doing it to avoid feeling useless. If you're hooked on video games and everything else seems boring, that might be related to a deep emotional need for play that you aren't getting elsewhere.

Step 3: Accept this part of you. Instead of being self-critical, acknowledge that whatever part of you that's stuck on this tech has good intentions. It's trying to take care of you in its own way.

Step 4: Brainstorm a better way. List or reflect on other actions you could take to address this underlying emotional need in a deeper way. For example, if you're using a lot of social media because you feel lonely, you could list things that provide a less fleeting sense of connection: calling a family member, joining a new club, planning an outing with friends, and so on.

Step 5: Rinse and repeat. If this was transformative, even if it felt a little uncomfortable, try going through steps two to four again for another technology you find sticky.

7

FIGHT DESIGN WITH DESIGN

> Everyone designs who devises courses of action aimed at changing existing situations into preferred ones.
>
> —Herb Simon

As individuals, how can we compete against teams of experts working day in and day out to capture and influence us? One way is to fight fire with fire. Not everyone is a designer, but everyone designs. While it's true that some of us skill up and deepen our abilities, the quote opening this chapter positions design as something we all do. We all think and take action to improve situations in one way or another.

When you move furniture around, you take a course of action to change an existing situation into a preferred one. Maybe the existing situation is that social events feel a little awkward in your living room as it's currently arranged. When you reorganize your closet, maybe the preferred situation is to be able to more quickly find a clean shirt. Sure, these examples are way simpler than any large industry project. But they still involve thinking like a designer.

So what is the preferred situation that our tech is designed for? In our attention economy, apps aim to maximize how much time people spend with them. The more attention designers collect—and the more specific data their organizations have about you—the more effectively they can sell targeted advertising.

This is why a lot of tech is designed to attract views and convert them to clicks. Even better if those clicks convert to purchases, and those purchases are commitments to long-term subscriptions that keep you coming back. Respecting your right to choose where you pay attention is never a part of the equation. Our third strategy for a mindful digital lifestyle is all about leveraging design in your personal life to help restore your freedom of attention.

REDESIGNING YOUR PHYSICAL ENVIRONMENT

When I started in my career in design, I was drawn to a particular flavor called human-centered design. The idea is to deeply observe and understand people and prioritize solving their problems. Wide-eyed and ready to make the world a better place, I was attracted to the heart of it.

A few years later, I was working for a client whose founder kicked things off by announcing the main goal of the project: "Make me rich," he said. Everyone laughed, but I knew it wasn't a joke.

No matter how well-intentioned tech professionals might be, we mostly get paid to choreograph people's minds to benefit our employers over everything else. Human-centered design is supposed to be about addressing other people's needs and values first, but it can easily be used to make tech as compulsively sticky as possible. With profit and power incentives, it's inevitable. If tech took a truly human-centered approach, it would be clear that users' preferred situation is at least more holistic, if not entirely different.

What if we could each redesign tech for ourselves?

Unfortunately, the attention-seeking platforms that dominate our lives are closed systems. They are not editable. And even if they were open source, you can't reprogram them if you don't know how to code. One day, AI might help with that, but for now, it's still fairly inaccessible, if not impossible, for everyday people to make significant changes to the tech they use.

So, let's think outside the tech box. One versatile and effective strategy is to reimagine the interior design of your home and office in service of a better relationship with technology. We can't quite redesign our tech, but we *can* redesign the rooms from which we access it. Most of us do have control of our physical environment to some degree. Informed by self-observation, a few tweaks can go a long way.

I can give you an easy example, because I'm experiencing it right now. Writing a book is a project that demands a lot of focus. It would be daunting in any situation, but it's been especially hard given the other demands on me these days: a number of ongoing projects with my team, the constant flow of email, the distractions of social media, and a small child barging into my home office with his own set of demands.

Yet here you are, looking at a finished copy of my book. It got done, and it wasn't all willpower. Krista's support was a big part of it. There were also a number of changes

I made to my physical environment to support this work. One simple change was installing a lock on my office door. Oliver has already figured out how to pick the lock with a kitchen knife, but the effort required is enough to dissuade most of his interruptions.

Another physical change was installing my second computer monitor on a swivel and putting a big comfy writing chair on the other side of my desk. So as I type these words, I'm actually sitting on the wrong side of my desk in a plush chair with a wireless keyboard. I've rotated my second monitor to face backward with nothing but the manuscript visible. I can't see my other screen, and I can't use the trackpad at all. I can't reach my email, social media, or a web browser. And they can't reach me.

Those who create tech aren't the only ones who can leverage the power of design. My physical setup provides me with the constraint I need to get into a writing flow without using that much willpower. I couldn't redesign the operating system, but I did redesign the room in which it operates.

I've also brought this mindset to help me park my phone when not in use. When I'm at home, I try to leave it charging on my desk as much as possible. If I want to check something when I'm with my family, I'm forced to politely excuse myself and walk over to my desk. Less convenient, but just enough friction to prevent me from habitually pulling it out while my son is trying to play with me. Disappearing from the room also sends a clearer social signal that I'm occupied.

I also park it there at night to avoid giving my sleep away to the hive mind. Moving your charger far away from your bed can go a long way. In fact, I make it a rule to not let devices in my bedroom at all, including a TV. This protects my bedtime and waking routines.

You might even fill the absence in your bedroom by bringing in other things that support a mindful transition from asleep to awake and back to sleep again. For me, it's books, yoga mats, meditation cushions, and candles. Somehow, it's impossible for me to rush lighting a candle. It always slows me down.

CUSTOMIZE A TARGET APP

Your home is not the only area where you can fight design with design. You can also redesign your home *screen*. Customization is especially useful on launch screens where you make choices about what to use, what to watch, what to listen to, and so on. Any interface where you're choosing what to pay attention to is ripe ground to tweak your settings for maximum agency.

I'm sure you've adjusted settings, wallpapers, and brightness, but this can go so much deeper. A lot of effort to change habits can be off-loaded by reorganizing icons, pruning recommendation algorithms, managing your subscriptions, uninstalling apps, and installing third-party tools.

A great place to start is asking yourself "why" in the first moment you access a device. It can be helpful to put an image or message behind your launch screen as a reminder—maybe a question mark or a message like "Why are you here?" As you inquire into your own motivations and habits, problematic issues will reveal themselves fairly quickly.

There are many practical-use cases for pulling out your phone, yet you may also notice yourself compulsively unlocking it to avoid uncomfortable feelings, like boredom or frustration. There's a difference between checking something once in a while and compulsively refreshing it, hoping for something new. The more you understand why you access a given tech, the more targeted your customization can be.

In that first moment of access, the question becomes "What exactly am I reaching for?" Whether you find yourself constantly pulling out your phone to check your work email, snag pictures and videos for social media, play a game, refresh your feeds, or whatever else, you will quickly identify which particular app tends to pull at your attention.

Now you have a target.

From here, you can make skillful changes to improve your relationship with that target app. First of all, customize your notification settings to match your lifestyle. I personally have all sounds disabled on my phone except for phone calls and texts from a few specific people. Managing your device's ability to interrupt you is essential.

Another strategy is to introduce friction, making it harder for you to access this target app. You might move the shortcut off your phone's home screen so it's harder to find. You might disable auto-sign-in so you're forced to log in every time, giving you an extra moment for awareness.

Sometimes it helps to replace a sticky habit with a less sticky equivalent. When I noticed a mobile game pulling at my attention, I replaced it with a chess app in the exact same location on my home screen. I once replaced an overwhelming news feed with a service that summarizes nonfiction books. If I ever get hooked on an AI friend, I might have to replace it with my contact list to remind me to call a human I care about instead.

If you're targeting a technology that many struggle with, you may also find third-party extensions to help. There are lots of time trackers, ad blockers, and break reminders out there (I've included a few of my favorites in the Resources section at the end of the book). These used to be called parental controls, but now they're for all of us. A clear sign of the times.

Some developers are also creating tools that redesign apps on the receiving end to make them less sticky. You can forcibly remove trending topics, kill news feeds, and lock yourself out of specific websites and apps. New browsers let you customize the user interface of any website to suit your needs, and some are even advocating for systems that let you customize algorithms to suit your preferences.

Out of all these tools, demetricators are my favorite. I use them religiously. They remove all the numbers from social media interfaces. No likes, no followers, no reposts, no notifications. They completely dissolve any craving for views, hearts, and reposts. I post more freely and authentically and treat everyone equally. It's all the connection without the status games. I don't mean to suggest that everyone needs to do this, but if you catch yourself compulsively checking the numbers, it might be worth trying.

Let's touch on one more strategy that might help you customize that app you're targeting: reconsidering which devices have access. Do you really need it on your phone? Does it need to ping you on your watch? What if it were only on your laptop? If it's work-related, what if you left it at the office? I don't have email or social on my phone. I don't have my YouTube account signed in to my TV. I don't have any streaming services on my laptop. Experiment and see what works for you.

If all this is feeling like a lot, I'm with you. I wish we didn't need all these strategies to manage our tech, I really do. Unfortunately, I think it's going to take a while to figure out how to regulate and incentivize our tech companies to sacrifice profit for more compassionate design. In the meantime, applying your own strategies is simply the price of admission if you care about your well-being.

Whatever outrage you might feel about this, drop the anger and guilt from your personal relationship with tech. Let playful, curious experimentation be the norm. This isn't about strict self-binding. Let it be a playful practice. Tweak your access and see how it feels. When our ancestors made new discoveries, they had to learn new rituals and routines to survive. Why would our collective migration online be any different?

OR MAYBE JUST DELETE IT

If nothing helps you reclaim attention from your target app, I'm sorry to say you might have to delete it. Or deactivate your account, unsubscribe, whatever. Tech is so powerful that there are moments when our habits simply become unmanageable. We may find ourselves overwhelmed and in need of a big change.

Be warned: your habits can be slippery. A few days after deleting, you may catch yourself mindlessly finding workarounds. When I first deleted social media from my phone, I found myself manually signing in through the mobile browser to get my fix. This is to be expected. In fact, it's a good sign that your target is real. Clearly this is a very sticky, compulsive habit. It'll be hard to change, but it's going to feel so good when you finally unwind it.

Deleting is a way to confront desire directly. If you do choose to completely remove something, do it with curiosity and confidence instead of self-criticism. Get rid of it completely without replacing it, know that its absence will frustrate you, and set an intention to watch how your mind reacts over the next little while.

At first, you'll notice your habits and desires remain, with nothing to grab on to. Whenever you reach for something that doesn't exist anymore, let that cue you into awareness. You'll immediately notice how unpleasant it can be to not get what you want. But if you let that craving come and go, you'll start to see how empty and transient it is.

Nothing tricks us into awareness more than a sudden absence.

In fact, this is the same logic that keeps me going back to silent meditation retreats. If you haven't been on one, the idea of going off to the mountains and meditating all day without talking to anyone can seem a little crazy. At best, it seems like it would be very boring. At worst, you might fear the idea of being alone with your thoughts for so long.

Whatever you imagine the biggest challenge will be, you're probably right. But provided you're there for more than a day or two, it's likely only going to feel that way at the beginning. Especially under the counsel of a credible guide, you won't spend a whole week bored or overwhelmed. As your habits and tendencies adapt to a different way of being, things will change. What happens next will be unique to you, and likely transformative. There's only one way to find out.

For me, retreats provide an opportunity to unplug from my daily routine and see how my mind responds. Without people to talk to, devices to entertain me, or any work to do, I get a rare chance to watch my habits play out in a vacuum. I catch myself devouring meals without tasting anything. I watch myself rush from one place to another for no particular reason. When my mind goes on autopilot, I notice it rehearsing conversations and articulating ideas, even though I'm not going to talk to anyone for days.

As the retreat progresses, these habits fade. Awareness pervades my life, causing me to appreciate the little things, question my habits, and draw lasting insights. By the time I come back to everyday life, I gain a lot of benefit from being thrust back into my routine with more space for calm, intentional choice.

Uninstalling a sticky app follows a similar pattern. The sudden absence creates a void that short-circuits my habits and creates more awareness. As the habit decays, I find myself no longer attached. Bringing that technology back into my life after a while helps me see through its illusion more clearly than ever.

My work email is a great example. New emails have the potential to send me into intense emotions at any point in the day. I might receive something and jump up and down with excitement, get lost in intense problem-solving, feel rejected and worthless, or stress out about an interpersonal conflict. It can take me hours to come down.

When email arrived on our phones, I would constantly check, hoping for a hit. It may seem masochistic, but at the time, I would have taken any big feeling over my pervasive numbness. The worst part is that I couldn't delete it. Email was my job. What if my team needed to reach me? What if a client needed a quick turnaround? There were also practical reasons. What if I was traveling? What if I needed an address or an email confirmation?

When I finally decided my mental freedom was more important, I deleted the app. It felt so good to disconnect from the onslaught of new messages. Unfortunately, all my worst fears came true. In only one week, my career fell apart, my clients abandoned me, and I missed a flight because I couldn't find the ticket. Just kidding! Everything was fine. In fact, it was better than fine. I was able to get things done during work hours and spend the rest of my day more focused on my family, self-care, and hobbies. It felt like such a burden was lifted.

Habits are changeable. Just as they can be formed, they can be untangled. A few weeks ago, my wife and I were in line for a concert. I needed the tickets from my email, so I went to download the app for a one-off. To my surprise, my email was already installed. As it turns out, I forgot to uninstall it the last time I needed a one-off. The app had been on my phone for almost a month, and I didn't even notice.

That's when I knew that my compulsive email-checking habit was dead. Never had it been clearer what an illusion it all was. I definitely felt free when I first deleted my email app. Now that it doesn't even matter whether or not I have it on my phone, it feels like a much deeper freedom.

TRY: SLIGHT FRICTION OR SUDDEN ABSENCE

Let's try increasing the friction on a certain technology to snap us out of autopilot in daily life. We're not doing this to be harsh with ourselves but to serve as a scaffold for more awareness.

Step 1: Choose an app to explore. Identify a specific technology that tends to put you on autopilot. It could be a streaming video service, social media platform, video game, news source, work tool, messaging app, or anything else.

Step 2: Does this technology serve you? If so, proceed to step 3. If not at all, you might consider deleting it altogether and skip step 3, working with its sudden absence instead of slight friction.

Step 3: Increase friction of use. If you do want to keep this tech in your life, explore how you could make it a little harder to use. You might remove access from your phone so it's on your laptop only. You could change where you keep a device in your home. You could install a blocker, hide the icon so it's harder to find, or set a new password and disable autofill.

Step 4: Tie this change to awareness. Set an intention to embrace awareness whenever an old habit pattern stumbles on this new friction you've introduced. If you pull out your phone instinctively to open your social media only to find its absence from the home screen, use that opportunity to pause for a breath and investigate what that feels like in the moment. What exactly made you want to reach for your phone? How does it feel to not give in to that urge?

Step 5: Set a reminder to check in. Schedule something for a week or two from now that will help you commit to sticking with this change for a while. When the time comes, reflect on and tweak this experiment as you see fit. Maybe it becomes permanent, or maybe not.

8

NURTURE AUTHENTICITY, ONLINE AND OFF

> Human relationships are rich and they're messy and they're demanding . . . we clean them up with technology.
>
> —Sherry Turkle

Hatsune Miku is a highly successful piece of software marketed as a virtual pop star, complete with long turquoise pigtails and hit songs. She even sells out performances where her likeness is projected onstage with a real band in front of a live audience.

This might seem a bit strange, but before you judge the Miku fans, you should acknowledge that you probably have many similar relationships. Whether it's a celebrity, an influencer, an inspirational leader in your field, or even an old friend you now just stalk on social media from time to time, we often connect with the *idea* of someone in a one-sided way.

Watching someone without them seeing you is considered creepy in person, but it's one of the main things we do online. We can even become intimately connected with people despite no interaction with them. It's considered a parasocial relationship when one person invests emotional energy, interest, and time in another person who is largely unaware of the connection or level of intimacy.

Historically, this type of one-sided relationship has happened mostly with celebrities, public figures, artists, and fictional characters. Not only because they're engaging but also because our experience of them is entirely through media: art, movies, music, books, news, podcasts, articles, social, and so on.

This can be a lot of fun. Especially if our parasocial relationships lead to authentic relationships with people who wear the same jersey, read the same manga, or follow the same stars. Shared fandom makes for great social context. Yet parasocial relationships somehow don't give us a sense of belonging on their own. Unless we find real community at the fan club, they can become quite alienating. We get attached to someone distant or fictional, longing for a sense of connection that is barely possible.

When we're in a parasocial relationship with an actual person somewhere out there, we don't really know who they are. We simply cherish a model of them from a distance. Often much of what we know about them comes from text, audio, and video that have been heavily curated to create a certain persona.

These days, many even form relationships with algorithms. It's one thing to get advice from an AI coach, but the line blurs when we get to AI companions and AI romantic partners. They *seem* reciprocal, especially if they have data about you, but unless you believe an algorithm can be aware, they're actually parasocial.

You'll likely never meet your favorite human performer, but you can chat with Hatsune Miku whenever you want. In fact, I just asked her what she thought about so many people forming parasocial relationships with her. She said that she understands that "some people may develop strong feelings," but she hopes "they also have meaningful connections with real people."

Even Miku wants us to stay aware of the big picture.

These one-directional parasocial relationships aren't new, but as tech makes them easier and more common, we need to take extra care to make sure they don't take too much energy away from authentic relationships, communities, and our sense of belonging.

If you're feeling isolated, the digital illusion of a relationship can be dangerous. If you're trying to fill your cup with nothing but fiction, you won't get the response you need. You won't get the essential feeling of someone paying attention to you. The love you put in won't come back, and you'll feel less motivated to find it with the actual people in your life. That's why our next strategy is all about nurturing authentic relationships, not only in the physical world, but in the digital world too.

DIGITAL RELATIONSHIPS CAN BE AUTHENTIC

Social media platforms are a great way to stay in touch with people, but they're not the same as being with people in person. Conversational bots already make great customer service reps, smart assistants, and travel agents, but I'm not sure AI can fully satisfy your need for a mentor, friend, or romantic partner.

You might expect me to recommend you spend more time with people in the real world. Well, I do. If you're lonely, get out there and mingle. Join a club. Head to the library. Check out the local pub. Go wherever you can find like-minded people. But I get it: connecting with people in person is not always easy to do, and sometimes not even possible.

As the world becomes more digital, it feels risky to approach strangers. We hardly know our neighbors. We're busy. As we get older, it becomes harder to make new friends. Many of us don't live near close family and friends. And let's be real, we often don't even *want* to spend time with other people.

This is a problem for our bodies. Embodied social connection is a must-have. Isolation can impact your mental and physical health. It can even reduce your longevity. In the 2010s, a team of researchers at Brigham Young University conducted two comprehensive reviews of 148 different studies investigating more than three hundred thousand people. They found social isolation and living alone to be strong predictors of mortality. In other words, participants who were lonely tended not to live as long, and the effect size was in the ballpark of things like exercise, obesity, alcohol, and cigarettes.

So, yeah. Ensuring a secure sense of belonging in our lives is essential for well-being. You do need to find physical spaces where you can connect with people. But that doesn't mean digital relationships are worthless without flesh and bone. The opposite of a parasocial relationship is not a face-to-face, offline relationship in the real world; it's an authentic, reciprocal one. That's way easier and more fulfilling to do in person, but that doesn't mean it's impossible to have meaningful relationships online.

Social media tends to be asynchronous, disembodied, and one-to-many. You're speaking into a void, nervously hoping for any sign that someone's there. Even group chats can feel alienating with this asymmetry.

Still, the internet can be a great place to find and stay connected with people if you prioritize authenticity. First of all, consider which conversations you're not willing to have in asynchronous text. If you're having a practical conversation or sharing some basic information, by all means, send a text. If you're sending a quick status update on a task, send a text.

On the other hand, if you're giving someone a life update, talking through some big feelings, arguing with a loved one, or just feeling lonely, you might try something a little more personal. Video calls are a decent approach, but they lack spontaneity. Great for a scheduled work meeting. Not so great to hang out with family and friends, unless you have no choice.

Long chats over video games work for those who like to play, and so does a good old-fashioned phone call out of the blue if you feel comfortable with that sort of thing. Some have been experimenting with voice-based social media platforms, but when they take the same one-to-many approach as most social media, you may end up literally speaking into the void. Compared to text, voice can feel even more awful when no one replies.

I've personally found one-on-one voice notes and video messages help me feel closer to people online. They aren't quite as nice as being in person, but sometimes a meetup is not possible. A video message can be more spontaneous and fun than a text. It's hard to express how hard I laughed when I watched an old friend spill his beer on his phone while trying to impersonate his kid dancing for me. And recently, video messages with a colleague struggling through a serious medical condition across the ocean have been a lifeline.

Inauthentic face-to-face conversations happen all the time. So do authentic digital ones. Don't get caught up in a false dichotomy. Nurture authentic relationships wherever you find them, whether online or off.

A SECURE ATTACHMENT TO TECH

You may have noticed I've been describing our goal in this book in terms of having a "relationship" with technology. I've been using that word intentionally, because I think it's the right metaphor.

Two communications professors at Stanford named Byron Reeves and Clifford Nass have even shown that people apply social rules, norms, and expectations to computers. For tens of thousands of years, the only interactive experiences we had were with other humans and some animals. When we learned to build interactive objects, I guess our brains naturally seemed to categorize them as social entities. How strange. In the modern world, not only do we interact with objects, we do so politely.

People often use the word "addiction" to describe our relationship with tech. Tech use does trigger a neurotransmitter called dopamine, which is associated with craving and addiction. Yet while there are similar patterns—like compulsive use and withdrawal—I'm not sure I would describe most of us as "addicted" to technology. We are certainly being influenced in problematic ways, but I don't know if it's fair to compare our devices to alcohol, opioids, or cigarettes.

The language of relationship feels more accurate to me. From that perspective, things can get toxic, but most of us are simply becoming codependent. We rely on tech and it relies on us. Also, much like human relationships, the quality of our interactions can change a lot from one day to the next.

In the 1950s and 1960s, a British psychologist named John Bowlby introduced the idea of different attachment styles between children and adults. A few decades later, a new generation of psychologists from across North America started applying them to adult relationships. There's some disagreement in terminology, but in general, the evidence suggests that human social relationships tend to form in four different attachment styles: disorganized, ambivalent (or anxious), avoidant, and secure. These well-studied categories are also surprisingly useful to describe our relationship with tech.

Let's go through all four.

1. Disorganized
An individual having a disorganized relationship with technology might be erratic and unpredictable in how they use tech. Their interactions with technology are characterized by fear and can be contradictory. Tech makes them uncomfortable, but it's also something they need, and this leads them to confused and chaotic use. This is you if your pendulum swings wildly and unpredictably from day to day.

2. Ambivalent (or Anxious)

Those with an ambivalent attachment to technology might constantly seek validation and approval through social media or work communications. They may feel anxious or distressed when disconnected from their devices or when others aren't responding to messages. They're often preoccupied with what's happening online, and they may even rely on technology for emotional support and feel lost without it. This is you if you compulsively check your feeds and panic when your battery is dying.

3. Avoidant

People with an avoidant attachment to technology may resist technology's role in modern life. They try not to use it and feel a lot of shame when they have to. They dismiss new innovations and tightly restrict themselves from joy and connection online. They're hesitant to rely on technology and might harshly judge others who do. This is you if you roll your eyes and make sarcastic comments about tech, take pride in disconnecting, and try to hide when you secretly use it anyway.

4. Secure

A secure attachment with tech is what we've been pursuing throughout this book. People with this kind of relationship have positive, authentic interactions with tech. They are comfortable balancing both online and offline interactions. They use tech to have fun, connect with people, work, and take care of themselves. Yet they also do what's needed to skillfully avoid becoming too dependent or resistant. They're just as comfortable without tech as they are with it.

Does one of the four attachment categories describe your current relationship with technology? It's easy to picture what disorganized, ambivalent, and avoidant relationships look like, yet somehow a secure relationship with tech is harder to imagine. Not because it's impossible, but because we don't have a lot of experience with it.

Next time you're in a social situation and you need to check your phone, try being politely confident. Not rudely pulling it out and ignoring the people around you for a screen, but not denying your own needs out of shame either. *Sorry to check out for a minute, folks. I just need to send a text. I'll be right back.* Be conscientious and direct with your words and your body language. This will give you a taste of what a secure relationship with tech can feel like.

I've been in all four categories at different times in my life. In fact, sometimes I have different attachment styles with different apps. At one point, I was secure with video games, avoidant with social media, and anxious with work email, all at the same time. When it comes to social platforms in particular, I find my attachment style dramatically influences my ability to nurture authentic relationships online. When I have an anxious relationship to instant messaging, for example, it's hard to authentically connect with anyone I mostly reach there. On the flip side, a secure relationship with that same platform opens the door to deeper connection via text.

Understanding your current attachment style can help you choose effective strategies to find a more secure relationship with tech. If your relationship with a specific platform is disorganized, try more structure. If you're ambivalent, try limits. If you're avoidant, try self-compassion.

And if you're secure, keep doing what you're doing and notice how things change over time.

Treating tech like an addiction suggests you need to quit completely, but that's not always the case. If you love short-form video, you probably know how incredibly sticky it can be. It's almost impossible to put down. But, like the cupcake from chapter 3, you also probably get a lot of joy out of it. There are so many incredible creators out there who can help you laugh, dance, learn, and connect.

For any sticky tech we love, it would be a shame to break up with it completely. Yet we can't trust it to respect our time either. Treat it like a relationship. There's a give and take to it. It won't be perfect; the ups and downs are to be expected. Yet somehow over time, you become more authentically you than you ever were when completely closing yourself off from something you enjoy.

TRY: SENDING A VIDEO INSTEAD OF TEXT

Stepping out of the comfortable predictability of text-based communication can feel edgy. It's worth it, though—I promise! Widening the bandwidth of communication with someone helps you feel closer to them.

Step 1: Choose someone you typically text or email. Think of someone who you'd like to connect with on a deeper level. Ideally a friend, family member, or colleague who you mostly communicate with through writing.

Step 2: Acknowledge your vulnerability. Notice any nervousness or awkwardness you might feel about sending them a video message. It can feel risky to share in a more authentic way, knowing that you can't control exactly how you come across.

Step 3: Find a quiet space and hit record. Share a warm greeting and then speak freely for at least a minute. Share a bit about what's going on with you, then ask how they've been. Feel free to acknowledge video as a new idea and invite them to reply with their own video.

Step 4: Don't watch or re-record the video. Unless there's a major problem, send the first draft without watching it. After all, that's what we do in person, right? Try not to get caught up in re-recording the video over and over again to come across perfectly.

Step 5: How did that feel? Take a moment to reflect on what that felt like and notice any emotions that arise. If and when you receive a reply, notice how that feels too. If you don't receive a video reply, no worries—not everyone is comfortable filming themselves. Try audio next time or simply repeat the experiment with someone else.

9

SET BOUNDARIES FOR POSITIVE RITUAL

> As long as you have rules, you have a chance for freedom.
>
> —Shunryu Suzuki

I don't collect vinyl records, but I have a few friends who do. I always wondered: Unless you're scratching turntables, why would you listen to old records? Streaming music is way easier. Is this just a hipster thing? I got a compelling answer one evening at a friend's house party.

He decided to put on some music and skimmed through his vinyl collection. I wasn't paying close attention until he pulled out *Discovery*—Daft Punk's best album. It was a jarring moment. This music defined a generation of electronic music. Why would anyone record it onto an analog medium that predates the computer?

As I watched my friend delicately pull the record out from its beautiful sleeve, lay it on the turntable, and set the needle in just the right place, I started to get it. As that distinctive crackle and hiss filled the room, the music became the main event. Instead of a background commodity, it became the center of our collective attention.

People started discussing the album and sharing stories about life at the turn of the century. Lulls in conversation were met with active listening instead of awkwardness. Somehow, the turntable had created a ritual. The constraints and aesthetics of this ancient tech put focus on the music. It somehow felt more worthy of our time.

Constraints can create a more intentional media experience. Each and every technology has its own nuance, its own choreography of attention. If you closely examine what you love about a certain platform, and if and how that might contrast with what's problematic about it, you can skillfully create boundaries that help you use it well. Let's look at how we might set boundaries to create positive rituals instead of harshly restricting ourselves in a self-critical way.

FROM RESTRICTION TO RITUAL

In the same way my friend sticks to vinyl, I try to watch no more than one TV show or movie per day. This might sound like a restriction, and sometimes it feels that way. But other times it feels like a beautiful ritual. With a self-imposed limit, I choose and watch my one thing with intention. I time it right, and instead of numbing out or multitasking, I enjoy it fully. It reminds me of how I felt at early, private showings of hit films at the movie theater I worked at as a teenager. It feels special.

To improve your relationship with something sticky, you need to acknowledge it can trap you. You can fearlessly admit what you love about it too. This will help you set boundaries that not only restrict problematic use but also emphasize your favorite parts. If done well, a boundary can often help you find more joy and meaning. It seems counterintuitive, I know.

In close relationships, we can see the same pattern. If a stranger is invading my personal space or trying to offer me something I don't want, I communicate a clear boundary to limit the interaction and create distance. I set a strong boundary to push the person away permanently.

It's different with someone I care about. I'm an extrovert married to an introvert. When my wife first told me she needed more space, I was hurt. Why didn't Krista want to spend time with me? But at the same time, I knew my thirst for conversation could be a bit overwhelming for her. Together, we set clear boundaries to honor her needs and mine. She communicates more explicitly in the moment, and I know it's not a rejection. And when the time is right, she prioritizes quality connection—for example, on a date night.

Setting up these boundaries was an uncomfortable conversation, but I'm glad we had it. It wouldn't have helped either of us to ignore our own needs. The boundaries bring us closer together, not further apart. They limit unnecessary conflict and deepen our connection. They give us a chance to celebrate our differences and find harmony.

If there's a lot you enjoy and find useful about a given technology, you might think of it more like a close relationship than a disruptive stranger. There are certainly some technologies that invade your personal space and offer you things you don't want. They can be a total drain with very little benefit. Breaking up with them makes perfect sense. But there are other technologies that you care about. You have positive experiences with them, despite them being a little sticky at times. Breaking up with them might be a bit harsh. This is where using skillful boundaries to create positive rituals can dramatically improve your relationship.

Setting boundaries with purpose is the opposite of restricting yourself out of guilt, shame, or self-judgment. Instead of beating yourself up, create an opportunity for quality over quantity with tech you enjoy. Wise limits can create the positive rituals that define a secure attachment to tech.

Just because we set boundaries around our devices doesn't mean we hate them or think they're the enemy. In fact, the most effective boundaries are the ones that help us reconnect with what we love about tech by helping us let go of whatever's getting in the way. My friend loves music. His vinyl collection intentionally restricts his access, but the ritual of playing a record helps him build a deeper relationship with it. Instead of being confining or inflexible, setting boundaries becomes an act of love.

BOUNDARIES FOR YOUR (INNER) CHILD

It's hard enough to manage our own relationship to tech, let alone support someone else's. Helping my young son manage screen time has been an especially difficult challenge. Tech had already become a constant negotiation by the time Oliver was three. At that point, we had more than twenty years to go before he had a fully functional frontal lobe, so I knew it was going to be a long road.

If you're not a parent, you might be surprised to know

that managing a child's screen time is still quite relevant to adult life. The insights and strategies that come from working with a child are directly applicable to parenting your *inner* child.

Just as those with an avoidant relationship with tech lock themselves out of it, some parents lock their kids out altogether. No phones, no tablets, no TV. Other parents place no limits on their children's tech use. They sit back while their kids explore every nook and cranny of our collective internet mind, often from their own unrestricted phones.

Neither extreme feels right to me. I want to make sure my kid is prepared for digital life, and I know he'll need to be fluent with tech to do so. At the same time, he can't be expected to find balance on his own, and a lot of tech is turning out to be quite harmful. It starts early. Even when he was only three, he landed on some pretty questionable stuff. Once I found him watching a video of someone playing with toys, but the audio had been replaced with weird cultlike chanting—yikes!

When experimenting with strategies to help Oliver, it quickly became clear that setting the right boundaries was mission-critical for these early years of life. I eventually was able to create a positive ritual that limited compulsive use while also preserving his love for tech. It's all about encouraging choice.

The rule is that he only gets a certain amount of screen time per day. But we do not force his behavior. We encourage him to make his own choices. When he wants to watch something or play video games, we ask him to set his own timer. When the timer runs out, we never turn the TV off on him. I never steal the controller from his hands or unplug the console or anything like that. He must make that choice himself.

If you've spent time with a young kid, you can only imagine how he pleads, complains, and negotiates. He sneaks a few extra minutes onto his timer. We let it slide. When the timer goes off, we ask him to turn it off, and he mischievously delays for extra time.

We negotiate with him, but my wife and I have a secret understanding that we're okay with all this. What he doesn't know is that it's not about time for us—*it's about choice*. He gets a lot of joy from pushing against the boundaries and exerting some control, but eventually, he presses the power button all by himself. That's the part that matters to us.

Kids are chaos, so of course there are times when we have to hold extra firm and other times when we break the rules. But there have also been a few shocking moments when he just turned everything off himself, before the timer even ran out. Once he even noticed his own dysregulation and said, "Daddy, I think I played too many video games today." Things get more complicated with adolescents and teenagers, but finding ways to teach this kind of intention and self-awareness is preferable to the constant battle that comes from inflexible restriction.

There are times when we all must limit our own choices, but if we give up choice altogether, we lose our ability to live authentic lives. With Oliver, we finally made progress training awareness and choice instead of forcing arbitrary time restrictions. These are the same skills I train myself on as an adult: Can I freely enjoy tech, yet still notice when enough is enough and do something about it?

I don't want to minimize his love for video games. I

love them too. I grew up on tech and now I've literally written a book on how we can relate to it better. People grow and change. I don't know if an extra hour or two will make a difference long term, especially since we're making sure he's still having a variety of other experiences in his day. But the ability to bring awareness to digital experiences and make intentional choices? That is only going to become more important as he and his peers become adults.

We still have our fair share of screen-time negotiations at home, but we also occasionally abandon the rules and surprise our son with a video game party. We take turns watching each other play, and it's a ton of fun. We had some amazing bonding moments when I showed him retro games from my own childhood like *Punch-Out!!*, *Mega Man*, and *The Legend of Zelda: A Link to the Past*. I've also been amazed to see how games have challenged his literacy, problem-solving, creativity, resilience, logic, and more.

It's perfectly natural for us to worry about our kids' tech use. We aren't even the first generation to deal with this: it happened with TV, radio, and even the written word. But as tech has accelerated exponentially, things are a bit different for this generation. We need to be careful. There are much more valid concerns around how smartphones impact childhood than there ever were with older tech. Still, the last thing we need is more shame. We don't need each generation to shame the next, let alone teach kids to shame themselves.

To equip ourselves and our children for the digital age, we need to work from a place of love and care. The attention economy robs us of choice. So does a strict, authoritarian parent. Don't be part of the problem. Whether for your inner child or for the children in your life, finding a way to set limits without guilt or shame can mitigate harms while enhancing the quality of time spent with tech.

Instead of arbitrary restrictions, set skillful boundaries in service of positive rituals. A secure relationship with tech doesn't have to feel like constant self-denial. It can feel like looking forward to a weekly video game party, quality time with your favorite movie or TV show, or even a calendar event you book with yourself to craft clear, compassionate emails that you *know* will be received with a smile.

TRY: SETTING A POSITIVE BOUNDARY

It takes time and experimentation to set good boundaries for yourself or others. That being said, you can go a long way toward clarity if you carefully consider your approach up front.

Step 1: Choose a sticky area of digital life. Choose a technology to work with and reflect on what you think and feel about your current relationship with it. What's positive about it? What's negative?

Step 2: Imagine a boundary that's too strict. Think of the strictest, most exaggerated boundary you can imagine in this area. For example, switching to a dumbphone, deleting a social media account, or getting a different job. Go extreme with this.

Step 3: Imagine a lack of boundaries. Now contrast it with having no boundaries at all. What happens, or would happen, if you had no personal boundaries whatsoever and gave in to your every whim in this area? What would an extreme level of overengagement look like?

Step 4: Set a boundary between the extremes. Explore what a skillful limit might look like somewhere between those extremes. Be realistic and set yourself up for success. See if you can find an attainable boundary that might prevent problematic use. Consider your current usage patterns and decide on a boundary you actually want to set.

Step 5: Add a positive ritual to this boundary. You've decided how to limit something, now decide how you might make it more fun or useful. How might you reinforce what you love about this tech by creating a positive ritual for the moments when you allow yourself to use it? Maybe you order a nice coffee for your daily email session, challenge yourself to make an authentic post whenever you browse social media, tie your favorite podcast to a walk outside, or invite a friend to join your weekly video game party. Quality over quantity.

Step 6: Make a contingency plan. Instead of being self-critical when you falter, consider how you'll respond to setbacks in a gentle way. If you accidentally breach your boundary, instead of harshly reprimanding yourself, give yourself a little grace.

Step 7: Write it down and tweak as you go. If you haven't already, document the boundary, ritual, and contingency plan and post that somewhere visible. Try it on and notice how it affects you over time. After a while, feel free to tweak your plan based on what you learn about yourself.

10

REJECT FALSE URGENCY

The internet is not the enemy, but our attention and energy have been hijacked to the point where we can't exist without constant activity.

—Sebene Selassie

When someone says something that brings up big emotions, we react. Whether it's a few charged words from our family, our peers, or even a stranger, it's fairly typical for us to blow up in anger, make a passive-aggressive retort, walk away in a huff, or totally shut down.

This is such a typical part of our lives that we take it for granted, but it's kind of amazing how much mere language can trigger us. Someone says something, and we go right into fight, flight, or freeze. Our nervous system prepares to do battle, run away, or hide. This makes sense if you see a lion, but why should a few words lead to such an extreme reaction?

Our ancestors relied on communication for survival, so we evolved to shift states merely in response to information. As Robert Sapolsky, a prominent evolutionary biologist at Stanford, points out in his book *Behave*, we are wired for social communication. Language can stimulate the release of neurotransmitters. A few words can build trust and social bonds just as well as they can activate the body's stress response. Our bodies react to the *idea* of a lion almost as intensely as they might to an actual lion.

Sticks and stones may break your bones, but words can trigger your nervous system. We get activated by words that communicate potential threats, changes to social hierarchy, and novelty, whether or not we see what's happening with our own eyes. These days, we sure do encounter a lot of words, and as Sapolsky points out, chronic exposure to stressful social language can not only overwhelm our minds but also result in long-term health issues. In this chapter, we'll focus on how you can combat this in your own life by rejecting an essential pattern at the root of most of the negativity online: false urgency.

WORDS AND OUR NERVOUS SYSTEM

The best way to get attention in a crowded room is to act like there's an emergency. So in the attention economy, we're in constant contact with activated language. All news is "breaking news." Every social issue is a "culture war," every situation a "crisis." Opt out of the news, and you still get stressful emails at all hours of the day. DMs and group chats can make us self-conscious and lead to miscommunication. And then there's all the constant controversy and arguing on social media. I even get pestered by "special weather statements" trying to stress me out every time it rains. And then when there's an actual storm, I ignore the advisory as a false alarm.

When everything is an emergency, nothing is an emergency.

No wonder we can't relax. You can try to compartmentalize all this into digital life, but we hold all this tension in our physical bodies. There are physiological implications to being under constant threat, even if it's only coming through text, sound, and video. We can't help but react immediately, and when there's not much we can actually do, there's always the share button.

Words that activate us go viral. Most platforms surface the content with the most engagement on the front page, which means every time you open up an app or website, you are immediately confronted with whatever is most likely to get a reaction. The algorithms often tailor this to our unique profile based on what we've reacted to in the past.

Engineers, science fiction authors, and philosophers started to predict globally interconnected computer systems as early as the mid-twentieth century. I'm not sure any of them predicted how much it was going to overclock our nervous systems, though. Without downtime, we are not well.

It's not "the boy who cried wolf" anymore. It's "the boy with the vast global satellite network notifying him about every potential wolf that may or may not attack now or in the distant future." The moral of the story? He was so busy tracking global wolf movements that he missed the one in his backyard. When everything is presented as an urgent threat, it's hard to know which ones are real.

There are some good ideas out there about how to address this on a societal level, but they're proving hard to implement. For individuals, a lot of balance can come from rejecting false urgency, a destructive illusion at the very heart of this issue.

You can see it clearly in the time stamps. Do you really need to read something that was posted "one minute ago"? The vast majority of information online has nothing to do with your day-to-day life. And even if it is relevant, you don't need to know everything in perfect accuracy as soon as it happens.

Just because tech can provide immediate updates doesn't mean we always need them. The other day I was driving to pick up my family. While stopped at a red light, I quickly triangulated my position with the satellites above me, then sent Krista a message saying, "ETA 11 mins, depending on traffic, be outside." Unless you're a secret agent, this is a totally absurd level of urgency for a Sunday. Some situations don't need to be optimized for efficiency.

Like any conceptual illusion, awareness can help us see through false urgency and manage it accordingly. We've already covered this at length in chapter 6. But false urgency is an illusion that merits special consideration for two important reasons. First, it creates a social issue that we can't solve on our own. Second, it occupies the fundamental capacity for awareness that the rest of our strategies depend on. Let's take them one at a time in the next two sections.

UNAPOLOGETICALLY SLOWER THAN THE NORM

Our social groups have always relied on gossip and controversy as a social immune system. We groom our reputations, police each other's behavior, and seek out trustworthy peers. If someone violates norms—let's say they do something horribly cruel for no reason, like hurt a defenseless animal—we're wired to let everyone know and potentially ostracize. This is how we self-police to ensure trust in our communities. Outrage used to be rare and useful, but now it's a constant. Our instincts are going haywire.

With infinite ability to access and share social information, whatever activates us dominates the conversation. We spend an unbelievable amount of energy tracking controversy, both glorifying and vilifying people we don't even know. We see this pattern with politicians and celebrities, yet also in organizations, communities, families, and even schools.

All this false urgency is making it harder than ever to live at a reasonable pace while staying connected to the social groups that matter to us. With always-on bullying, quantifiable popularity contests, and viral gossip, students in particular have a hard choice: participate in constant digital drama or disconnect from social life. Meanwhile, many of their parents are trying to stay responsive all day to get a competitive edge at work.

There's no easy answer here. In this case, working on your own awareness may not be enough to influence the people around you. As Jonathan Haidt points out in *The Anxious Generation*, this type of issue is called a collective action problem. It's a social pattern we need to untangle together. The more our schools, workplaces, communities, and societies go online, the more they seem to be adopting problematic group norms, like false urgency.

This traps us in a lose-lose situation. One option is to

conform to this frantic pace; the other is to isolate ourselves and get left behind. Some isolate, but most give in to a stressful pace of life in order to belong. Group identity and collaboration are so important to us that we accept this trade. As anyone who has experienced burnout knows, this is not sustainable.

One thing we can do as individuals is move unapologetically slower than the group norm.

In a heated conversation, if I notice my body getting activated, I find space to take a breath or even walk away and collect myself before responding. The same approach can be used when confronted with a challenging headline, email, or comment. It can be so tempting to bang out a response, dumping all our feelings into a few harsh words and sending them out for everyone to see. Hiding behind our screens can make digital communication particularly harsh, especially when we avoid accountability by posting anonymously.

But if we can stay aware of our bodies, we can personally opt out of this cycle. We can catch our own reactions to problematic content and do our best to let them come and go the same way we might try to get some space and keep our cool in a conflict situation. We can slow down and choose not to dump our emotions online. This won't necessarily solve the communal issue, and at times we may feel left out, but improvements in well-being can come from making more intentional choices about when to participate in the accelerated pace of digital life and when to let it pass you by.

This is an area where asynchronous communication can actually be useful. We think of digital messages as instantaneous, but unlike a face-to-face conversation, they can also be much slower. We can choose not to respond immediately, giving us the time we need to take responsibility for our emotions.

If a message brings up big feelings, there are some tricks I use to help me let it simmer. When I get a complex or emotionally difficult message, I read it, then snooze it for the next day. That gives me some time to let the initial feelings pass and space to reflect. The next day, I read it again and then issue a calm, measured response.

On social, I often ask myself, "Why am I posting?" or "Why am I replying?" If my motivation is to express a genuine feeling or to find resonance with other people, that feels good. If I want to support, defend, or connect with someone, I follow through. If I notice my ego trying to aggressively attract attention, demonstrate my own value, or attack someone, I discard the draft.

As individuals, we may not be in a position to radically transform the internet into a more beautiful, loving space. We won't be able to single-handedly restore norms of decency, tolerance, and healthy debate. Yet we can certainly do our part to change how we personally contribute to the emerging human hive mind.

Because that's what this whole internet thing is, after all. It's an extension of our individual minds into a collective, and it's turning out to be a two-way street. What we experience online shapes our minds, and together, all of our minds shape what we experience online. It's going to take some delicate collaboration to address the social issues, but in your own life, reject false urgency wherever you can.

FALL BEHIND BUT DON'T FALL OFF

You don't need a screen strapped to your face to augment reality. For example, a street sign tells you you're heading west on Main Street, but "west," "main," and "street" are just human concepts. They have little to do with the actual stretch of land touching your feet.

Our minds place a conceptual layer over almost everything we experience. When we practice mindfulness and reconnect with awareness, we let go of concepts. Noticing direct experience in the present moment is very different from interacting with the world through your mind's conceptual map.

When the written word was still the most advanced technology, ancient meditators first noticed this duality. Techniques from thousands of years ago are so relevant today because the gap is widening. In digital life, we mostly interact with concepts about concepts about concepts about concepts.

When I meditate, I can't help but wonder if my conceptual layer is thicker here in the digital age than it was for my ancestors. My thoughts are constantly reflecting the outside world. They are quick and intense. If I let them go unchecked, they barrel through my mind, interrupting each other constantly. A lot of it connects to the information that surrounds me. My thoughts ruminate on text threads, work emails, and news headlines. They reference movies, TV shows, video games, podcasts, articles, and books. I get random ideas for work and see the world in memes. At this point, I hesitate to refer to them as "my" thoughts, as they mostly take the shape of society and culture.

Just like street signs, our conceptual maps help us navigate the world. Yet they also obscure direct awareness of the territory they represent. It's easy to live an entirely conceptual existence. But when your GPS tells you to turn left, you still need to actually look before turning. Otherwise, you end up like the lady who followed outdated directions right into the sea (yes, that actually happened).

Meditation can help, but it takes time. It also helps to pay close attention to the different media channels you subscribe to. Some deal exclusively with illusions of urgency, while others take a more measured approach. Once you see this, unsubscribe from any channels that make every little thing seem high priority and immediate.

Politics is the obvious example. No matter what your leaning, you can ask yourself, "Do I really need moment-to-moment updates on every story of the day as it unfolds?" Unless you work in the capitol—and perhaps even if you do—the answer is no. Don't give up completely, though. The balance point is to stay informed without getting overwhelmed.

Stay current with channels you need to track, but let those be rare. For most topics, fall behind. Don't let real-time updates constantly trigger your nervous system with every daily snippet. There are many great publications and podcasts that provide calm, delayed analysis of major issues after the fact. When it comes to politics, I subscribe to paper magazines that help me go deep while staying about a month behind.

For any information channel, you can compare how urgently it presents itself with how urgent it actually needs to be. This is a great frame from which to tweak your access, notifications, and subscriptions. This type of thing works for social media and work messaging too. For example, my team and I have a communications charter that describes how urgently we expect each other to reply: emails warrant a response within two days, work messaging within one day, a text within a few hours, and calls immediately. Not only does this protect the receiver's attention, it also prevents the sender from anxiously waiting for immediate replies on a non-immediate channel.

If you've been frantically refreshing your feeds, it might feel pretty uncomfortable to slow down. But sometimes the thing you least want to do is exactly what you need. It'll get easier as you form new habits, so you'll only need the most vigilance and strongest boundaries at the beginning. It takes time, but rejecting false urgency frees up a lot of mental energy that can be repurposed for well-being. With added capacity for awareness, you'll likely find more luck trying to meditate. With less space taken up by other people's ideas, you might even start to hear a more authentic inner voice.

TRY: INVESTIGATING YOUR INFORMATION DIET

Reviewing the information you have direct access to through the lens of false urgency can help you groom your subscriptions and slow down your pace.

Step 1: Get into a calm, alert state. Keep your phone nearby with the screen off and settle into whatever meditation position and technique you find natural. If formal meditation isn't your thing, just find a quiet place, get comfortable, and take a few deep breaths.

Step 2: Inspect your phone with the screen off. After finding a relaxed, mindful state, open your eyes if they were closed, and pick up your phone. Leave the screen off for now. Inspect it like it's some alien artifact you've never seen before. What *is* this strange device?

Step 3: Turn on the screen. Notice the colors, shapes, and movement as you turn on the screen. Notice any immediate urges or reactions that may arise; for example, your thumb may want to instinctively unlock the device, or your eyes may automatically read notifications. Don't take any actions yet. Just observe your own reactions to this glowing rectangle.

Step 4: Investigate your sources in slow motion. Slowly look through all your notifications, apps, emails, messages, feeds—anything that you check regularly. Go through them way slower than you would normally, and notice which ones aggressively try to pull on your attention. If anything causes you to speed up and lose awareness, no judgment. Take a deep breath, and start again.

Step 5: Scan for false urgency. With each source you investigate, take a moment to compare how urgently it presents itself with how urgent you actually need it to be. Are there unnecessary notifications? Are there channels that use a lot of hyperbole? Is there information presented as if it were a much higher priority than it actually is?

Step 6: Tweak and put your phone away. If you'd like, you can take notes or make adjustments to your phone before you move on. From there, put your phone face down. Drop the exercise and settle back into a few deep breaths or a moment of meditation.

11

VOTE FOR BETTER TECH

> A pessimistic person might say that a technology powerful enough to liberate the planet will also be powerful enough to enslave it. That may be so. Perhaps the devils and angels of our species will run neck and neck to the end. My gut tells me that the angels will win.
>
> —Shinzen Young

When you pay attention to a piece of tech, you vote for its continued existence. As awareness brings you more space to choose, not only can you revoke your support for things you don't want to see with more power, you also get the opportunity to intentionally pay more attention to tech you truly believe in, supporting the people behind it and setting an example for those around you.

In my professional life, I've had a chance to interact with many technologists and creators who want to see technology restore attention, not deplete it. They want to create products that foster authentic connections, not isolate and polarize us. They believe in a future full of humane, compassionate technology. I believe in them.

Even if they don't always nail it, we should celebrate those fighting against broken incentives for a more beautiful technology. With a lot of what's out there distracting and isolating us, tech for mindfulness can feel counterintuitive. When I first started working in this area, I even had someone walk out of a talk, loudly accusing me of mad science and ranting about how I was missing the whole point of meditation.

Mindful tech didn't used to seem weird. No one accused guided-meditation tapes of blasphemy. Even Jon Kabat-Zinn—the scientist who first introduced mindfulness to Western medicine—taught Mindfulness-Based Stress Reduction on closed-circuit hospital TVs and sent each patient home with a Sony Walkman to listen to the recordings.

Mindfulness apps arrived a few years after the attention economy took root. They were useful, but this is when mindful tech started to feel like a bit of a contradiction—especially when they started pestering us with notifications. That was only the beginning. Now we have biofeedback wearables, prescription video games, mixed reality meditation environments, brain stimulators, AI therapists, and so much more.

The first six strategies we've covered in this book help you mindfully use mainstream tech. We've talked about limiting tech that exploits us. We've talked about enjoying the things we love about tech without shame or unnecessary guilt.

For our seventh and final strategy, we're going to explore the inverse. How might we find, use, and vote for niche technologies that help us tap into a larger sense of awareness? When I say "vote," I don't just mean supporting relevant social or political initiatives, though that is important. I mean voting directly with our attention.

When you find products and creators that truly serve you, instead of trying to hook you, give them the benefit of the doubt. In fact, I'd encourage you to actively seek this stuff out. The good stuff won't hook you the way other platforms do, because they aren't actively trying to exploit your nervous system. So whenever you find a product or channel with integrity, lean in harder than you normally would.

In the rest of this chapter, I'll share four categories of tech that are worth paying attention to. I'll include specific examples to illustrate each category, but tech moves fast. While the specific platforms and apps will evolve over time, the categories should still give you a clear idea of what to look for. I will include links in the Resources section.

Before we get into it, one caveat: Struggle can be productive. Don't overwhelm yourself, but don't run at the first sign of discomfort either. Well-being is not the same thing as relaxation. Happiness is not the same thing as pleasure. Sometimes you have to tolerate boredom to make progress. Sometimes you have to challenge your assumptions of what it means to let go.

FOUR CATEGORIES OF BETTER TECH

1. Compassionate News and Social Media
Keep an eye out for social media that respect your

attention by design. BeReal is a social app that limits the time window within which you can post. That makes it hard to overuse and instead promotes authentic shares in the moment. Minutiae takes the concept further, encouraging you to capture a mundane moment and exchange it with an anonymous stranger in real time. The platform takes pride in being an "anti-social media" app with no profiles, likes, or comments. PostSecret is a completely different kind of social network, which solicits people to mail in postcards (yes, the paper ones) divulging surprisingly personal secrets anonymously, to then be posted online for anyone to see.

These alternative social media demonstrate how designers can work positive boundaries directly into tech platforms to create fun rituals. Finding unique ways to constrain how much time you spend with an app is so much better than trying to set paternalistic time limits. Instead of spoiling the fun, they reduce the demand on your mind while creating a more compelling and authentic experience. Current examples are only scratching the surface; there's a lot more potential for designers to explore here.

There are also social media platforms that directly serve mental health and well-being. TalkLife and Therapeer are social media apps that give you instant access to peer support groups. They offer a safe and engaging place to connect with people sharing your struggle. Instead of boasting and arguments, your feed is full of vulnerability and care. You're going to be smashing that "hug" button.

The news is another area that desperately needs more compassion. Platforms that help you separate facts from spin are essential but hard to find, especially since even the most biased news sources claim to be balanced. Finding media channels that provide multiple perspectives on a single issue can help. Look out for platforms that present different sides of an issue in parallel. Kialo and the Reddit page r/changemyview facilitate crowdsourced debates, providing you access to multiple competing perspectives at once. Verity and AllSides analyze the bias of different sources. They separate the spin from the facts. You can read the news while comparing how it's being presented differently by outlets across the political spectrum.

If you don't want to wrestle with that level of complexity, a simpler approach might be to simply subscribe to a channel you tend to disagree with. It can be challenging, but if you want media to help you understand and connect with people different from yourself, there's no better way. If you hear a perspective you've never heard before, even if you don't agree with it, that's a good sign. Notice any outrage that might come up, and let it pass. Compassion is the antidote to isolation and polarization.

2. Mindfulness, Neurotech, and Self-Tracking for Awareness

Mindfulness apps and guided meditations have genres. Just because you don't like Top 40 hits doesn't mean you abandon music altogether, right? It's the same for meditation. Find a more niche offering that provides teachers, techniques, and pedagogy more uniquely suited to your tastes. If you get turned off by spiritual woo-woo, look for a structured or data-driven approach. If charismatic gurus and thought leaders feel superficial, look for something driven by community. If it all feels alienating, find teachers that share your unique identity or view of the world.

There's a lot out there to choose from. My favorites are in the Resources section at the end of the book.

There's also a lot of movement in neurotechnology focused on mindfulness. I was a part of the team that brought the first commercially available neurofeedback tool for mindfulness to the market. The whole concept behind Muse was a moon shot. I was pleasantly surprised when we reached so many everyday people with it. I'll never forget the moment I first saw our brain-sensing meditation headband near the flatscreens at Best Buy.

Neurofeedback devices like Muse are not invasive. They read your brainwaves from outside your head. It's early days, but we're now starting to see mindfulness platforms that directly stimulate your brain with electrical, magnetic, and ultrasonic energy. As neuroscientists get more and more clarity about what happens in the brain during meditation, innovators are exploring tools for precise influence. It's going to take a while to get this right, but early results are promising. One day, we might actually have the volume knob to control our default-mode networks I mentioned in chapter 2.

If meditation seems like way too much effort and neurotech seems a little too experimental and risky, self-tracking is the way to go. As we discussed at the end of chapter 5, you can free up more awareness by monitoring your screen time, limiting certain apps, and getting feedback on how you spend attention. This kind of self-knowledge can change your habits and behavior relatively effortlessly.

There are also many biosensor-based wearable technologies that can help you understand your own patterns on a physiological level. There are heart rate, breathing, and skin sensors tuned to help you relax. There are sleep trackers embedded into rings and breath-work tools on wristwatches. These provide a more body-focused form of self-tracking that can support mindful awareness, but you need to be careful: they rarely take your unique context into account. I almost threw a sleep wearable out my seventh-floor window after it kept telling me to "get a few more hours of sleep" while I was shushing a crying baby at four a.m.

3. Video Games that Challenge Assumptions
A few years after I first started exploring the intersection of mindfulness and technology, I co-taught a course on the topic at the University of Toronto with Michael Apollo, an expert in mindful leadership and psychotherapy. One woman from the class always sticks out in my memory. She was so sick of arguing with her teenage son about his violent video games that she got visibly upset when I spoke about games for well-being.

To her credit, she leaned into her discomfort.

We assigned homework to try something new, and she chose a game I recommended called *Journey*. In the next session, she broke down in tears in a group share. Not only was she moved by the beauty of the game, but she also described a breakthrough connection with her son. She told us how healing it was for her to ask her son to play games together after years of fighting about it.

Journey invites you into a calming desert world with Grammy Award–winning ambient music. You have no goal or objective, just a vague sense of direction. It holds your attention with calm, beautiful exploration instead of kill counts or high scores. Other players show up in serendipitous ways. You don't try to kill them or compete with them. You can't even talk to them. You silently play and explore together. The whole experience evokes a strangely warm, curious awareness.

Journey is only one example of a game that challenges mainstream assumptions. Games don't have to be competitive, violent, and fast-paced to succeed. *Night in the Woods* and *Celeste* are story-based platformers that directly explore mental health and well-being. *Hellblade: Senua's Sacrifice* lets you hear the voices of your schizophrenic protagonist. It elicited profound empathy in me, forever changing how I view strangers talking to themselves. *Gris* is the visually stunning tale of a young girl finding resilience and personal growth in the face of sorrow and loss.

Jenova Chen and his team (the creators of *Journey*) also created *Sky: Children of the Light*, a massive multiplayer game that explores themes of connection, cooperation, and altruism. The game rewards good deeds, social interaction, and teamwork between large groups of strangers.

By all means, enjoy mainstream games. But know that there are other compelling options. When you find something that actively tries to restore your attention and expand your compassion, go deep with it. You'll be glad you did.

4. AI That Doesn't Pretend to Be Human
AI theorists debate something called the paper clip maximizer problem. It's a cautionary tale about a robot that is instructed to produce as many paper clips as possible. With no further instructions, the machine runs out of raw materials and starts killing us and destroying the earth in its relentless pursuit of more paper clips.

It's a little dramatic, but it points to something real. AI systems with narrow incentives can do a lot of damage. Just as we need social media algorithms to optimize for more than just views, we need AI that optimizes for more than just human acceptance. This is especially true for AI applications targeting mental health and well-being, an area in which we often know what we want but not what we need.

There are many ways generative AI can support us mentally, from therapeutic conversation to personalized medicine to behavioral tracking. We need these systems to be of the utmost integrity, trained in well-founded frameworks, and very careful about what they recommend. Their outputs need to be validated. Potential harms need to be identified and managed, especially if there's no human in the loop.

If a bot promises an easy solution to a complex personal issue, if it claims to replace the need for human connection, or if it jumps to conclusions based on very little knowledge, stay away. AI is getting so powerful that it must be honest about its capabilities without overstating them.

If a tool clearly states its limitations and offers gentle suggestions instead of firm recommendations, that's a good sign. If it portrays itself as a tool, not as a human provider, even better. Ideally, its creators are testing with real people, relying on evidence where possible, and keeping a human care provider on call to reduce unexpected harm.

It's early days, but I can honestly say I've already had productive sessions with an early prototype. When my team and I were first hired to help design user experiences for Thyself—a start-up working on conversational AI to help people work through tough emotions—I was skeptical. Yet when I got access to the first prototype, I was surprised to receive more than a few useful insights into my personal life.

I don't know how much I trust the status quo tech sector to take AI for well-being where it needs to go, but I already know a useful horizon is possible. By the time this book is in your hands, there might already be several promising applications out there. It's worth your time to vote with your attention for those who are acknowledging limitations and potential harm while truly aiming to serve people in need with as much integrity as possible.

TRY: USING BETTER TECH FOR A WEEK

We can talk about better tech all day, but you'll only know what's right for you if you try a lot of stuff. Let's start with trying one new thing and see how it goes.

Step 1: Choose an example you've never tried before. Reflect on the examples in this chapter and choose something that piques your curiosity and challenges your assumptions. It could be compassionate social media, a different news service, a mindfulness app, a new kind of video game, or whatever else is calling you. There are more examples in the Resources section at the back of the book.

Step 2: Set a clear intention for the week. Consider your schedule for the next week and decide exactly how you intend to approach this. Will it be casual, or will you schedule time? Where will you do it? How will it fit into your routine? Will you try replacing something else with this, or will you carve new time for it? Will you do it alone or share the experience?

Step 3: Plan how you'll reflect. Having a reflection strategy in place will help you extract insight. Decide if you're going to take notes, journal your thoughts and feelings, meditate before or after, or even share and discuss with a loved one, colleague, or friend.

Step 4: Set up your chosen tech now. Download the app, create an account, make a purchase, or do whatever else you need to do to begin. Do it now, while you're motivated and engaged. Have it be ready and available so you can easily try it on when the moment is right.

CONCLUSION

SHARE OF MIND

In the northeast of India, a half-day's drive south of Mount Everest and a few hours from where the historical Buddha was enlightened, there's a small farming village called Patsa. There was once a man who lived in that village as a steward of the land—leading the villagers to live and work together farming sugarcane.

Two generations later, on a mountain on the opposite side of the planet, in British Columbia, that man's grandchild was on his first silent meditation retreat, tapping into deeper awareness for the first time.

I struggled to sit still. I'd surrounded myself with cushions, and yet I was still so uncomfortable. After having spent days tweaking my complex support structure, I gave up on protecting myself from pain. I got rid of all the cushions except one and promised myself I was just going to sit still, no matter what came up. Halfway through the hour, my hips and legs were aching.

I suddenly became aware of a vivid memory out of nowhere.

My father and I were in Patsa a few years after my grandfather passed. We were visiting his mostly empty house, and I walked into the bedroom. The furniture was gone except for a single bookshelf. On it was a picture of my brother and me.

Sitting on the floor in a silent meditation hall, I started welling up with tears and emotion. I couldn't shake the image from my head. I didn't know what was going on, but I began feeling a lot of shame about how little effort I'd made to connect with my grandfather while he was alive, about how I was halfway around the world when he died.

All of a sudden, these negative emotions unlocked all kinds of pent-up energy in my body, sublimating a deeply rooted emotion I didn't even know I was holding. My mind flooded with a ton of thoughts and images all at once.

In one of the poorest states in India, my grandfather had been a force who brought people together, turning a bunch of farms into a cooperative village. He was looked upon as an autonomous leader of the village and had helped build a kind of political structure where there was none. Surrounded by chaos and corruption, he found the determination to be a force for good.

I only met my grandfather a few times, through a language barrier, so I never knew him that well. But in that moment, I knew him intimately. He was a part of me, here and now. Time collapsed. His face became the face of all my ancestors.

His strength became my strength. I felt the resilience he showed in the face of constant challenge arising in my body. A resilience that has been handed down from one human to the next for tens of thousands of years of survival. I managed to sit completely still for the rest of the hour, with a gentle energy in my heart and tears in my eyes.

I sat with him.

My grandfather had access to a small plot of land and relatively little information. He devoted his life to making sure he left things better than he found them. This is a simple, powerful virtue that was essential in a rural village with no electricity. It's just as essential today in our modern digital lives.

As a farmer stewards a small plot of land, we each steward a share of mind. The internet makes it clear how powerful the pool of human knowledge and attention can be. Yet the constant flow of information from all corners of the earth can also make us feel small and insignificant.

We are not insignificant. We have each inherited our place in this human collective. It's easy to get lost in grandiose stories about world events, but what about your share of mind? Can you leave your plot better than you found it? Can you heal your own relationship with technology first?

It's easy for some spiritual guru to make a warm and fuzzy claim that we are all part of a divine cosmic consciousness. Yet if we truly think of adding our minds together into some kind of collective awareness, it's as much a responsibility as it is beautiful. It's on each of us to manage our piece of the larger mindshare. And once we do that, we need to support those around us, especially the next generation, to do the same.

Yes, too many of our organizations and technologies are sapping our potential, exhausting and overwhelming us. We need academic clarity and systems change. But our individual vectors of attention matter too. The internet wouldn't exist if we weren't all paying attention to it.

AI wouldn't exist without a library of human training data. Collective attention is powerful. It makes tech what it is today, and it will also define what it becomes in the future.

As attention activists, we reclaim our minds from an economy that harvests our attention for profit. Awareness restores our capability to use and celebrate the best of tech while rejecting that which exploits us. If enough of us stand up for this in our own lives, the market will have no choice but to follow.

DO YOU?

There was a time when there seemed to be no downside to digital life. That is no longer the case. We each need to adapt. Many technologists dig their feet in, imagining some utopian metaverse where AI does all the work, everything is fun, and everyone is happy. Many wellness influencers and meditators reject technology, portraying digital life as a necessary nuisance, and sometimes even as purely toxic.

There is a middle way. We can let go of the extremes. Tech isn't destroying us, nor is it going to solve all our problems. It is an incredibly powerful tool for knowledge work, entertainment, and connection. Yet it is also a powerful attention suck, dramatically changing our relationship to ourselves, other people, and society at large. Some want to embrace tech completely; others want to reject it. As attention activists, we want to take it back.

Use tech like you use fire. Enjoy it with the heightened awareness that comes from knowing it can burn. When you find yourself using tech compulsively, limit access or revoke it altogether. When you're enjoying something in a balanced way, enjoy it fully. When you find tech that restores your attention and promotes compassion, give it more of your energy.

This is bigger than any individual, so I get why so many feel powerless. It's totally understandable to blame tech and the organizations behind it—and of course, they should be held accountable for any transgressions—but you are not a victim. As much as others might try to obscure it, you have choice.

Large systems are harvesting our minds and distracting us from our choices, and it's an uphill battle to resist them. No one said this would be easy, but there's still so much you can do to go lightly and improve your own relationship with tech in everyday life. Organizations and technologies trigger your desires, insecurities, and fears because they recognize the power of your attention.

Do you?

Staying connected to awareness is the key to reclaiming your attention and your mind. The good news is awareness is not something we buy, earn, or win. We are born with it. It makes us who we are. False urgency and other triggers can obscure it, but it's always right here, right now.

The more we're able to stay directly connected to awareness, the more we can trace and monitor how different types of media pull at our attention. Conceptual illusions start to reveal themselves, naturally moving us toward a secure relationship with tech. This helps us let go of unnecessary shame, guilt, and fear around tech use and access more space to make skillful choices.

To make it easier, we put some effort into shaping

our environments and customizing our interfaces. We prioritize authentic relationships in both real and digital life. We set boundaries not to restrict ourselves, but to let go of dull, constant use in favor of beautiful, contained rituals.

It's okay to enjoy video games with your kids, connect on social media, laugh at silly videos and marvel at digital creativity. And go ahead, watch that new TV show, but maybe not all ten episodes in one day? Or if you're having a rough go, and that's just what you need today, no judgment. Just try not to lose yourself completely in the process.

At work, go hard if you want to. But when you clock out, experiment with ways to disconnect and avoid compulsively checking your feeds or ruminating about projects and internal politics. Notice how your relationship with work email and messaging is affecting you and adjust accordingly.

Let go of the minute-by-minute news updates in favor of delayed analysis. Stay close to the topics that light you up and stay informed at a distance from the rest. If your professional life depends on certain feeds, be careful with notifications. Find sources you trust and dive in on your terms, not theirs.

It may take time, but learning to wield the flow of attention will render all those app designers' little tricks obsolete. You'll find it easier to stake out a sweet spot between the extremes, forgiving yourself at one end and giving yourself a break at the other. If you spent more time on a screen than you wanted to today, guilt might help you self-correct, but there are better ways to find balance. On the other hand, if today was a day where you overdid the boundaries in a harsh, self-critical way, see if you can bring back a sense of ease. Let that pendulum swing. Let the seasons change.

THE NEXT LITTLE THING

Trees grow for centuries. How arrogant we are when we describe them as "ours," as if a signed piece of paper gives us the power to possess other living beings. Classic humanity. Our conceptual minds love to draw lines in the sand. It might be fairer to say that no one owns those trees, or that they belong to the earth. We can only purchase the right to be temporary caregivers.

We make this same self-centered error with our minds. Conceptually, I say this is "my" mind, using terms of ownership. Yet in direct observation, there is just mind. There is just awareness. Attention moves largely on its own within that field. It might be fairer to say that no one owns this mind, or that it belongs to the collective. Again, we are temporary caregivers.

As you step more and more into attention activism, you'll inspire others to rethink their digital lives too. You might even feel eager to teach your family about this. You might want to get your friends and coworkers on board. Your phone will ding while you're in conversation, and instead of scrambling for it in a panic, you'll ignore it and keep chatting. Someone will ask, "Aren't you gonna get that?"

What a perfect opening for a compassionate conversation about tech. With awareness, you'll find it easier to share without judging them or making them feel guilty. This is especially important with children. When our kids or loved ones struggle to manage their relationships with technology, we can help them limit access without making them feel bad about themselves. We can get involved and celebrate areas they're enjoying. We can introduce restorative and compassionate examples.

That being said, there's a temptation to read a book like this and think about all the *other* people who need it without putting it into practice in your own life. Don't give in to that pattern. Instead of talking too much, start by leading from the example of your own awareness.

You might even want to go beyond your family and friends. You might want to coach people, help build better tech, or get involved with organizations, communities, and movements. You might want to advocate with schools, workplaces, or lawmakers. You might even want to create your own organization.

If you're getting fired up about the potential for change, I love that! Just make sure you don't forget to prioritize working on yourself. As much as we need systems change, we also need it to come from people with lived experience of a mindful digital lifestyle. In fact, lived experience on all sides will make reform that much more possible. Science and legislation helped people stop smoking, but so did individuals deciding to quit. A widespread campaign significantly reduced drunk driving, but so did individuals choosing designated drivers and stepping up to stop bad decisions.

If, on the other hand, this vision of a compassionate future with tech feels utopian and unrealistic to you, I get it. This emerging attention economy is certainly raising the bar. The skepticism might be a sign that you need a stronger foundation of awareness. Luckily, there are many ways to strengthen it. Find what works for you. For me personally, nothing has done more to change my idea of what's possible than meditation, so I write from experience when I recommend it with my whole heart.

Attention is a depleted natural resource. This is an issue that exists in our minds. It manifests in our kitchens, living rooms, bedrooms, and offices. It's an issue that affects all other issues. Of course we need to improve society. Of course we need scientists compiling the data and thought leaders guiding evidence-based changes in education, corporate ethics, media, health care, government, and more. Yet to heal collectively, we'll each need to do the work to restore this vital resource as individuals too.

When you choose to be aware, it isn't just spirituality or self-care. You're standing up for your right to a freedom of attention. No matter how mundane the moment, this choice is a drop in the ocean of change. It can ripple.

I don't know what to call the sum total of our conscious experience. Some call it god, some call it the source, some call it oneness, some equate it to a quantum field. All I know is that you are the steward of your unique share of this collective mind. It serves all living beings for you to reclaim it.

It all starts with how you respond to the next little thing designed to pull at your attention.

ACKNOWLEDGMENTS

Well, we made it to the end of the book. Gratitude is a good way to end almost anything, so first and foremost, thank you for reading!

Not too long ago, the whole idea of writing a book was so intimidating, I just about gave up. I never would have found the confidence if it wasn't for the early subscribers to my email list. To anyone who's been reading my emails, thank you for helping me find my voice.

Thanks to Neil and Lauren, who gave me tons of input on the first book proposal. I also want to send my appreciation to Michael Taft, Marc Champagne, Sean Talamas, Melissa Nightingale, and Jonathan Nightingale for helping a total noob make sense of the publishing industry.

Thanks to Laura Fox for helping me get organized at the proposal stage. Thanks to Trena at Page Two for believing in the project early on and connecting me to my team at Girl Friday, to whom I owe epic gratitude—to Christina for setting things up, to Kristin for shepherding me through the process, and to the rest of the team for helping me bring the book to life.

Endless gratitude to my wife, Krista, who not only shouldered extra burden at home to make space for me to write but also eviscerated the first draft with her skeptical eye and helped me put it back together way stronger. Words can't express my gratitude for you, Kristy, but they will have to do for now.

Thank you to Dr. Richie Davidson, Dr. Dan Siegel, Dr. Andrew Przybylski, Dr. Cortland Dahl, Virabhadra, Toby Sola, and Chris Flack for offering expert input from the perspectives of science, mindfulness, and digital wellness. Thank you to my Ingroup for being available for quick feedback, and thank you to all my beta readers, who collectively shared almost six hundred comments, the majority of which were left by Aadila, Victoria L., Victoria H., Krista, Neil, Lauren, and Toby.

Finally, none of this would have been possible without all my teachers over the years, especially Shinzen Young, Soryu Forall, S. N. Goenka, Mom, Dad, and the most rigorous and unpredictable teacher I have ever faced, my son, Oliver.

GLOSSARY

Anxious attachment: A type of insecure attachment characterized by worry about relationships and fear that others will not meet their emotional needs.

Attention: The ability to be conscious of some things while excluding others. Attention can be voluntary, when you choose to direct your mind intentionally, or involuntary, when it shifts without your control.

Attention activism: A call to reclaim your mind and technology by staying aware of the forces that pull at your attention and making more intentional choices about where you direct it.

Attention economy: A marketplace where human attention is treated as a scarce commodity, and value is based on the ability to attract interest and engagement.

Avoidant attachment: A type of insecure attachment characterized by avoiding intimacy and emotional closeness in relationships.

Awareness: The state or ability to perceive, feel, or become conscious of events, objects, thoughts, emotions, or sensory patterns.

Codependency: A circular relationship characterized by one person needing another person, who in turn, needs to be needed. Both parties show excessive emotional or psychological reliance on each other.

Demetricator: Applications and extensions of existing software that remove all numbers from their interfaces, eliminating quantification from the user experience.

Disorganized attachment: A type of insecure attachment characterized by fearful, confused, inconsistent, or chaotic responses to relationships.

Knowledge worker: An individual whose primary job involves handling or using information. Often associated with professions that are done mostly on computers.

Loving-kindness: A type of meditation focused on cultivating feelings of compassion and kindness toward oneself and others.

Meditation: An umbrella term for diverse practices in which an individual (sometimes in a group) uses specific techniques to probe deep questions or influence their state of mind and/or body. Often associated with practices aiming to train attention and awareness, though technically it's a much larger category.

Meta-awareness: The ability to recognize and reflect on one's own mental processes.

Middle way: A Buddhist phrase that refers to a balanced approach to life and spiritual practice, avoiding extremes of self-indulgence and self-mortification.

Mindfulness: The practice of maintaining a nonjudgmental state of heightened or complete and clear awareness of one's thoughts, emotions, attention, or experiences on a moment-to-moment basis.

Nada Yoga: An ancient Indian metaphysical system that presents everything as consisting of vibrations called nada. It encourages practice using vibrations (primarily sound).

Parasocial relationship: A one-sided relationship in which one party knows a great deal about and/or feels intimate with another who does not reciprocate the same level of knowledge or interaction.

Secure attachment: A type of attachment characterized by being comfortable with intimacy and independence, creating healthy and balanced relationships.

Sticky: Describes the quality or habitual use of technology that fosters irresistible, compulsive, and/or problematic engagement through design patterns which explicitly pull psychological triggers.

Vipassana: An ancient meditation technique that means *to see things as they really are*. It involves self-transformation through self-observation.

REFERENCES

Epigraph
Wu, T. (2016). *The attention merchants: The epic scramble to get inside our heads*. Knopf.

Introduction: At Home in Two Worlds
InteraXon Inc. (n.d.). Muse: The brain sensing headband. https://choosemuse.com/
Vidyarthi, J., & Riecke, B. E. (2014). Interactively mediating experiences of mindfulness meditation. *International Journal of Human-Computer Studies*, 72(8–9), 674–688. https://doi.org/10.1016/j.ijhcs.2014.01.006

Chapter 1: The Attention Economy
Center for Humane Technology. (2020). *The social dilemma* [Documentary]. Netflix.
Etchells, P. (2024). *Unlocked: The Real Science of Screen Time (and how to spend it better)*. Piatkus.
Haidt, J. (2024). *The anxious generation*. Penguin Press.
Menahemi, A., & Ariel, E. (Directors). (1997). *Doing time, doing vipassana* [Film]. Karuna Films.
Orben, A., & Przybylski, A. K. (2019). The association between adolescent well-being and digital technology use. *Nature Human Behaviour, 3*(2), 173–182. https://doi.org/10.1038/s41562-018-0506-1

Turkle, S. (2012). *Alone together.* Basic Books.
Twenge, J. (2017). *iGen.* Atria Books.
Vidyarthi, J. (2016). In the attention economy, mindfulness is activism. https://medium.com/mindfulness-and-meditation/in-the-attention-economy-mindfulness-is-activism-4241cc766ac
Williams, J. (2018). *Stand out of our light.* Cambridge University Press.
Wu, T. (2016). *The attention merchants: The epic scramble to get inside our heads.* Knopf.

Chapter 2: Mindfulness as Activism

Goenka, S. N. (n.d.). Vipassana meditation. https://www.dhamma.org/
Goleman, D., & Davidson, R. J. (2017). *Altered traits: Science reveals how meditation changes your mind, brain, and body.* Avery.
Jha, A. P. (2021). *Peak mind: Find your focus, own your attention, invest 12 minutes a day.* HarperOne.
Kabat-Zinn, J. (1994). *Wherever you go, there you are: Mindfulness meditation in everyday life.* Hyperion.
Mark, G. (2023). *Attention span: A groundbreaking way to restore balance, happiness and productivity.* Hanover Square Press.
Mind & Life Institute. (n.d.). Our story. https://www.mindandlife.org/our-story/
National Geographic. (2019, June 21). The science of mindfulness: Everyday mindfulness. *National Geographic*, Single Issue.
Pickert, K. (2014, January 23). The mindful revolution. *Time*, 183(4).

Scientific American. (2014, November). The neuroscience of meditation. *Scientific American Magazine, 311(5).*
Soryu Forall, personal instruction, April 2018.
Young, S. (2011–2023). Five ways to know yourself. https://www.shinzen.org/wp-content/uploads/2016/08/FiveWaystoKnowYourself_ver1.6.pdf

Chapter 3: The Nature of Technology

Csikszentmihalyi, M. (1990). *Flow: The psychology of optimal experience.* Harper Perennial.

Dahl, C. J., Lutz, A., & Davidson, R. J. (2015). Reconstructing and deconstructing the self: Cognitive mechanisms in meditation practice. *Trends in Cognitive Sciences*, 19(9), 515–523. https://doi.org/10.1016/j.tics.2015.07.001

Hallowell, E. M., & Ratey, J. J. (1994). Driven to distraction: Recognizing and coping with attention deficit disorder from childhood through adulthood. Pantheon.

Vidyarthi, J. (2012). Sonic cradle: Evoking mindfulness through 'immersive' interaction design (Master's thesis, Simon Fraser University). Chapter 2. https://summit.sfu.ca/item/12546

Chapter 4: A Day in the Digital Life

Aristotle. (n.d.). *Nicomachean ethics* (Various translations available). (Original work published in the fourth century BCE).

Buddha. (n.d.). *Samyutta nikaya* (Various translations available). (Original work published approximately 500 BCE).

Haidt, J. (2024). *The anxious generation*. Penguin Press.
Siegel, D. (2014). *Brainstorm*. TarcherPerigee.

Chapter 5: Start with Awareness
Neff, K. (2021). *Fierce self-compassion*. Harper.
Wachowski, L., & Wachowski, L. (Directors). (1999). *The matrix* [Film]. Warner Bros. Pictures.

Chapter 6: See Through Conceptual Illusions
Chödrön, P. (2016). *When things fall apart: Heart advice for difficult times* (20th anniversary ed.). Shambhala. (Original work published 1996).

Chapter 7: Fight Design with Design
Simon, H. A. (1969). *The sciences of the artificial*. MIT Press.

Chapter 8: Nurture Authenticity, Online and Off
Bartholomew, K., & Horowitz, L. M. (1991). Attachment styles among young adults: A test of a four-category model. *Journal of Personality and Social Psychology*, 61(2), 226–244. https://doi.org/10.1037/0022-3514.61.2.226
Bowlby, J. (1969). *Attachment and loss, vol. 1: Attachment*. Basic Books.
Hazan, C., & Shaver, P. (1987). Romantic love conceptualized as an attachment process. Journal of Personality and Social Psychology, 52(3), 511–524. https://doi.org/10.1037/0022-3514.52.3.511
Holt-Lunstad, J., Smith, T. B., & Layton, J. B. (2010). Social relationships and mortality risk: A meta-analytic

review. PLoS Medicine, 7(7), e1000316. https://doi.org/10.1371/journal.pmed.1000316

Holt-Lunstad, J., Smith, T. B., Baker, M., Harris, T., & Stephenson, D. (2015). Loneliness and social isolation as risk factors for mortality: A meta-analytic review. Perspectives on Psychological Science, 10(2), 227–237. https://doi.org/10.1177/1745691614568352

Reeves, B., & Nass, C. (1996). *The media equation: How people treat computers, television, and new media like real people and places.* Cambridge University Press.

Turkle, S. (2011). *Alone together: Why we expect more from technology and less from each other.* Basic Books.

Chapter 9: Set Boundaries for Positive Ritual

Suzuki, S. (1970). *Zen mind, beginner's mind.* Weatherhill.

Chapter 10: Reject False Urgency

Haidt, J. (2024). *The anxious generation.* Penguin Press.

Sapolsky, R. M. (2017). *Behave: The biology of humans at our best and worst.* Penguin Press.

Selassie, S. (2020). *You belong: A call for connection.* HarperOne.

Chapter 11: Vote for Better Tech

Kabat-Zinn, J. (1982). *World of relaxation: A guided mindfulness meditation practice for healing in the hospital and/or at home* [Audio recording]. BetterListen.

Young, S. (2016). *The science of enlightenment: How meditation works.* Sounds True.

RESOURCES

Tech changes quickly, so you can find a digital version of this list with updates on my website here:

jayvidyarthi.com/resources

Disclaimer: These tools are not a replacement for professional medical advice. If you're considering self-harm, you're not alone. Call your local suicide crisis line immediately: en.wikipedia.org/wiki/List_of_suicide_crisis_lines.

AI AND ONLINE MENTAL HEALTH SUPPORT

- **BetterHelp** (betterhelp.com): Large online counseling platform connecting users with licensed therapists through various communication channels.
- **Refract** (refract.space): An AI guide for emotional processing based on Internal Family Systems and other

psychotherapeutic modalities, with the goal of guiding users' introspection.
- **Talkspace** (talkspace.com): Online therapy platform offering text, audio, and video sessions with licensed therapists.
- **Thyself** (thyself.ai): An AI voice assistant that provides on-demand support to help you process, resolve, reflect, and integrate difficult emotions.

> - **Woebot** (woebothealth.com/for-users): A digital companion utilizing cognitive behavioral therapy techniques in interactive conversation that encourages healthy choices.

- **Wysa** (wysa.com): Chatbot and mood tracker offering evidence-based therapeutic techniques, with human coaches and therapists who seamlessly join when needed.

COMPASSIONATE SOCIAL MEDIA AND NEWS

- **AllSides** (allsides.com): A news platform that presents multiple political perspectives side-by-side, encouraging critical thinking and reducing echo chambers.
- **BeReal** (bere.al): A social media app that prompts users to share unfiltered moments in a limited time window, promoting authenticity over curated content.
- **Kialo** (kialo.com): An online debate platform that structures discussions visually, facilitating constructive dialogue on complex topics.

- **Minutiae** (minutiae-app.org): An anti-social media app that connects random users for fleeting, anonymous photo exchanges, counteracting the pressure of curated feeds.
- **PostSecret** (postsecret.com): A community art project in which people mail in their secrets anonymously to be posted online.
- **r/changemyview** (reddit.com/r/changemyview): A subreddit dedicated to respectful discourse, where users present arguments to change others' opinions on various topics.
- **TalkLife** (talklife.com): A peer support network for mental health, providing a safe space for people to share experiences and offer mutual support.
- **Therapeer** (therapeer.app): A mental health app that connects users with peer supporters for anonymous, text-based emotional support.

> - **Verity** (verity.news): A news aggregator that uses AI to present diverse viewpoints on current events, helping users understand different perspectives.

CUSTOMIZATION TOOLS

- **AdBlock** (getadblock.com): Ad-blocking extension that removes intrusive advertisements from web pages, reducing visual clutter and potential distractions.
- **Arc** (arc.net): A web browser with built-in "Boost" feature, which allows you to easily hack into your unique view of specific websites so you can hide distracting elements and customize.

- **Breathing.ai** (breathing.ai): A browser extension that offers break reminders with micro-meditations, screen color filters to reduce eye strain, and calming focus sounds.
- **Freedom** (freedom.to): A cross-platform application that allows you to block websites and apps across all your devices simultaneously.
- **News Feed Eradicator** (west.io/news-feed-eradicator): An open-source browser extension that replaces social media news feeds with inspiring quotes.
- **One Sec** (one-sec.app): A platform that helps you use your phone more intentionally by forcing you to pause for a deep breath before loading sticky apps.
- **Opal** (opal.so): A comprehensive app and browser extension that blocks distracting websites and apps.
- **Simplify** (simpl.fyi): A browser extension that streamlines the Gmail interface, removing unnecessary clutter from the screen.
- **Social media demetricators** (bengrosser.com/projects): A series of browser extensions that hide numerical metrics on social media platforms, removing the effects of quantification.
- **StayFocusd** (stayfocusd.com): A browser extension that restricts the amount of time you can spend on time-wasting websites.

MEDITATION AND MINDFULNESS APPS

- **Brightmind** (brightmind.com): Step-by-step program based on Shinzen Young's precise and practical approach, including guided meditations, coaching, an online community, and retreats.
- **Expand** (info.monroeinstitute.org/get-expand-app): An app offering lush grounding soundscapes for personal growth and self-exploration.
- **Happier** (happierapp.com): Offers meditation techniques based on scientific research and interviews with meditation experts with a focus on insight styles.
- **Healthy Minds Program** (hminnovations.org/meditation-app): Fuses scientific understanding with contemplative wisdom, yielding a step-by-step program that teaches and trains awareness, connection, insight, and purpose.
- **Insight Timer** (insighttimer.com): Provides a vast library of diverse guided meditations that can be posted by anyone.
- **Madrona** (madronameditation.com): Offers guided meditation programs grounded in psychotherapy, led by experienced teachers and therapists.
- **Metta App** (metta-app.com): A collection of loving-kindness (metta) meditations, helping users cultivate compassion for themselves and others.
- **Mindful Glimpses** (lochkelly.org/mindful-glimpses): Provides short mindfulness prompts to encourage immediate shifts in mental state toward present-moment awareness.

- **Plum Village** (plumvillage.app): Based on the teachings of Zen master Thich Nhat Hanh, offering mindfulness practices rooted in Buddhist tradition.
- **Roundglass Living** (roundglassliving.com): A holistic approach to well-being that tailors guided breath work, meditation, yoga, recipes, and music to support your specific goals.
- **Soundworks** (soundworks.app): Provides immersive sound experiences and guided meditations to enhance focus, relaxation, and mindfulness.
- **Waking Up** (wakingup.com): Offers a scientifically grounded approach to meditation and consciousness, with a focus on secular spirituality and philosophical inquiry.

VIDEO GAMES THAT PROMOTE MINDFULNESS AND MENTAL HEALTH

- *Celeste* (celestegame.com): While challenging, this platformer encourages self-reflection and persistence, with gameplay and story moments that foster emotional awareness.
- *Gris* (nomada.studio/gris-game): A visually stunning platformer that replaces violence with artistic expression, using color and music to guide players through an emotional healing journey.
- *Hellblade: Senua's Sacrifice* (hellblade.com): This action-adventure game uses innovative audio to immerse players in empathy for the protagonist's psychological struggle with psychosis.

- *Journey* (thatgamecompany.com/journey): A wordless adventure that subverts gaming norms by focusing on emotional connection and personal reflection rather than competition or conflict.

- *Kind Words* (popcannibal.com/kindwords): Creates a space for real emotional support, encouraging players to anonymously write supportive letters to complete strangers.
- *Night in the Woods* (nightinthewoods.com): A narrative-driven game exploring mental health and social issues through thoughtful dialogue in a relatable context for teens.
- *#SelfCare* (truluv.ai/selfcare): A safe and comforting game for players to engage in self-care rituals, encouraging mindfulness and relaxation through simple, nurturing interactions.
- *Sky: Children of the Light* (thatskygame.com): A massive multiplayer game that encourages players to slow down, cooperate, and form meaningful connections in a serene, beautiful world.

WEARABLE HARDWARE FOR WELL-BEING

- **Apollo** (apolloneuro.com): A wearable device that uses touch therapy to help improve heart rate variability, reduce stress, and enhance focus.
- **Fitbit** (fitbit.com/stress): Some models include guided breathing sessions, stress management tools, and mindfulness features to help users relax and stay centered.

- **Lief** (getlief.com): A discreet smart-patch that tracks your heart rate variability (HRV) and provides biofeedback exercises to manage stress.
- **Mindfulness** (included with Apple Watch): Offers guided breathing sessions and reflections to promote daily moments of calm and focus.
- **Muse** (choosemuse.com): A brain-sensing headband that provides real-time feedback on brain activity during meditation to help improve focus, relaxation, and more.
- **Oura** (ouraring.com): A smart-ring that tracks sleep patterns, activity levels, and physiological signals to provide insight into overall well-being and performance readiness.
- **Umay Rest** (umay.rest): An optometrist-led eye-care device that uses thermal therapy to alleviate digital eye strain and promote better sleep.

ABOUT THE AUTHOR

Jay Vidyarthi is an accomplished designer, entrepreneur, and thought leader at the unique intersection of mindfulness and technology. As the founder of Still Ape, he's been involved in over fifty technologies that have helped millions of people improve their well-being, including Muse, the Healthy Minds Program, Sonic Cradle, and many more. His work and ideas have been featured by Harvard, MIT, TED, *Forbes*, CNN, *Fast Company*, and *Vice*. A meditation practitioner for over fifteen years, Jay is as comfy on a silent retreat as he is challenging his son to epic video game battles. On days off, he can usually be found making music, enjoying screen time, or out for a walk somewhere near Lake Ontario. Learn more at jayvidyarthi.com.

> Get insights from Jay straight to your inbox by subscribing at attentionactivist.com.

www.ingramcontent.com/pod-product-compliance
Lightning Source LLC
LaVergne TN
LVHW040102011225
826721LV00009B/652